THE BOOK ON ADVANCED TAX STRATEGIES

THE BOOK ON ADVANCED TAX STRATEGIES

Cracking the Code for Savvy Real Estate Investors

VOLUME 2

AMANDA HAN AND MATTHEW MACFARLAND

BiggerPockets®
PUBLISHING
Denver, Colorado

Praise for the Series

THE BOOK ON TAX STRATEGIES FOR THE SAVVY REAL ESTATE INVESTOR

THE BOOK ON ADVANCED TAX STRATEGIES: CRACKING THE CODE FOR SAVVY REAL ESTATE INVESTORS

"There's a saying: It's not how much you make, it's how much you keep—and there are few places where this is more applicable than real estate investing. In this book, Amanda and Matt explain the tax benefits of real estate in a way that even the most novice investor can understand, and they give both new and seasoned investors alike the tools necessary to put these strategies to work to start saving money immediately. This book is a must for any investor's bookshelf."

—J Scott, Author of *The Book on Flipping Houses* and co-host of *The BiggerPockets Business Podcast*

"You can't even get your CPA to listen to your voicemail message for the cost of this book!"

—Brian Burke, CEO of Praxis Capital

"Matt and Amanda are top-notch professionals with whom I have been associated for many years. Their clientele demands answers to the most current changes in the tax code, and their new book gives all of us a big advantage in creating strategies that will save us money and help keep our wealth!"

—Bruce Norris, Real estate investor, philanthropist, and host of the award-winning *Norris Group Real Estate Radio Show*

"The only certain things in life are death and taxes. Thankfully, Amanda and Matt have made the latter much less of a sure thing! This book has a down-to-earth yet informative style that makes it fun and easy to read, while also helping to save real estate investors BIG money."

—Brandon Turner, Bestselling author of *The Book on Rental Property Investing* and co-host of *The BiggerPockets Podcast*

"If you want to learn how to embrace the tax code and make it work for you instead of against you, this book is a must read. With *The Book on Advanced Tax Strategies*, you don't have to fear tax time or feel hopeless about the checks you'll write to the government each year. This is a brilliant tool that will help you keep more of your hard-earned money!"

—Elizabeth Benton, Business owner, podcaster, and bestselling author

"Matt and Amanda knocked this one out of the park! [They] lay out a... clear understanding of the rules of self-directed investing, whether in an IRA or in a Solo(k). The book goes deep into the upside of tax-free and tax-deferred retirement savings as they illustrate the financial benefits. Want to invest your retirement funds outside of Wall Street? Read this book first!"

—Kaaren Hall, CEO of uDirect IRA Services, LLC

The Book on Advanced Tax Strategies: Cracking the Code for Savvy Real Estate Investors, Volume 2
Amanda Han and Matthew MacFarland

Published by BiggerPockets Publishing LLC, Denver, CO
Copyright © 2020 by Tax Strategies Institute, LLC
All Rights Reserved.

Publisher's Cataloging-in-Publication data

Names: Han, Amanda, author. | MacFarland, Matthew, 1975- author.
Title: The book on advanced tax strategies: cracking the code for savvy real estate investors / by Amanda Han, CPA and Matthew MacFarland, CPA.
Description: Denver, Colorado: BiggerPockets Publishing, [2019] | Includes bibliographical references.
Identifiers: LCCN 2019034495 (print) | LCCN 2019034496 (ebook) | ISBN 9781947200227 (paperback) | ISBN 9781947200289 (ebook)
Subjects: LCSH: Income tax—United States. | Real estate investment--United States. | Income tax deductions—United States. | Taxation—United States. | Real estate investment—Taxation—Law and legislation—United States—Popular works.
Classification: LCC HJ4653.R4 .H36 2019 (print) | LCC HJ4653.R4 (ebook) | DDC 343.7305/246—dc23
LC record available at https://lccn.loc.gov/2019034495
LC ebook record available at https://lccn.loc.gov/2019034496

Published in the United States of America
Printed in the USA on recycled paper
10 9 8 7 6 5 4 3 2 1

MIX
Paper from
responsible sources
FSC® C008955

This book is dedicated to:

Our parents,
without whom none of this
would have been possible.

And to our kids,
who we hope to raise with
the belief that anything is possible.

TABLE OF CONTENTS

INTRODUCTION
CRACKING THE TAX CODE

Tax law is convoluted and getting more complicated every day. Try reading the Internal Revenue Code for ten minutes and you will feel like Alice in Wonderland chasing a rabbit down a rabbit hole. People often ask us why the tax law is so complicated.

The reason for the complexity of our tax code is that it was not designed simply to collect tax revenue—the truth is, our tax system was designed with many other goals in mind as well. Besides raising revenue, taxes are designed to both stimulate the economy and to influence social behavior. Tax benefits are provided to those who exhibit the intended behavior, while tax hurdles exist to discourage people from unwanted behavior. Investing in real estate is one of the behaviors that the government wants to encourage, so the tax code is filled with benefits and loopholes that incentivize us to use real estate to grow our wealth.

Contrary to popular belief, having a higher income doesn't have to mean paying more in taxes. You may have heard that Amazon, the world's largest retailer, paid zero income taxes in a year when it earned $9.4 billion in net profits. This didn't happen by chance—it was achieved with careful planning and utilization of the many loopholes that the government intentionally created for taxpayers. Amazon operated their business to stimulate the economy in the way the government intended, and as a result, the company was able to pay zero taxes. In other words, there is nothing illegal about making $9.4 billion in profits and paying no taxes. If companies like Amazon can control how much tax they pay, how can we as real estate investors do the same?

This book is designed to help answer this exact question. Believe it or not, tax breaks are not just for the multi-billion-dollar companies and the millionaire investors. Tax breaks exist for people from all walks of life, all types of professions, and all income levels.

During speaking events, we meet many real estate investors with all types of backgrounds—from newbie investors looking for their first deal to seasoned investors with dozens of properties. We meet active investors involved in wholesale or fix-and-flip projects, as well as investors putting together syndications of large multifamily or commercial deals, and we truly enjoy speaking with them about their investments, strategies, and goals.

Without fail, investors ask us questions they have about their own taxes. It's extremely surprising to us that—even though most Americans know that the tax code favors real estate investors—most investors have no idea how to actually take advantage of these benefits. What can they deduct as real estate expenses? Why did their CPA say a home office is not available for real estate investors? Do they really need an LLC to take advantage of the real estate write-offs we shared from the stage?

When we wrote our first book, we intentionally chose topics that would be easy to explain. Our goal was to help investors build a solid foundation and understanding of some of the strategies that can be applied to everyday real estate investors. Of course, we could not end the story there. As real estate investors, it is important to take the next step toward more advanced tax-saving strategies. After all, why pay Uncle Sam more than required when the tax code is filled with loopholes for real estate investors?

Since the strategies discussed in this book may be more advanced, we have tried to simplify the calculations and scenarios as much as possible without losing any of the content. Our hope is that, regardless of your experience level in investing and taxes, you can find some golden nuggets here to help you save taxes year after year. As you will see in the real-life stories in this book, some of the strategies can help an investor create thousands—or even hundreds of thousands—of dollars in tax savings.

The book is not designed to make you a tax expert, but to provide enough information so that you can ask your tax advisor the right questions. Then you can have productive and strategic planning sessions to see how these strategies apply to your situation.

Let's face it: Taxes are not a sexy topic. In fact, the majority of Americans despise taxes and everything related to taxes. Although we can all agree that no one is thrilled to "pay" taxes, people dread taxes for many other reasons. Tax rules are thorny—many people have a fear of the tax code because of its complexity. Preparing for taxes can be tedious and time intensive. Although we file taxes every single year, preparing to do them can feel like a whole new learning process every time. Between understanding what we can deduct, which documents we need, and how to best organize the information, tax time can be a nightmare. Even after spending all that time, many of us may feel helpless and uncertain whether all that work actually helped to reduce our final tax bill.

For most taxpayers, the fear of taxes results in a vicious cycle. We dread taxes, so we try not to think about taxes. As a result, we may not spend the time needed during the year to capture and track legitimate deductible expenses. The year goes by, and we realize once again that we cannot hide from Uncle Sam after all. So, in early April, we're extremely stressed because we now have a very limited amount of time to get our income and expenses together before we need to meet with our tax preparers. We try our best to dig up receipts and throw them together quickly. Because we did not track our expenses throughout the year, we lose out on a lot of legitimate tax deductions because we simply cannot remember everything we spent money on during the past year.

As a result, we end up with a large tax bill, just like the year before. We painfully write that check to the IRS and promise ourselves we will do better next year. It's yet another horrible tax filing experience, and as we leave our tax preparer's office, we let out a sigh of relief. Thank goodness, taxes are finally done, and we don't need to worry about them until this time next year....

If you can relate to this, you are not alone. This is the relationship that the vast majority of individuals have with taxes. Our goal in this book is to help you think differently about taxes and tax planning. We want to demonstrate that, as real estate investors, you can use specific strategies that are designed to help you take control of your tax bill and keep more of your hard-earned money.

We know that the tax man comes around each and every year. So instead of burying our heads in the sand and waiting until the last minute to confront the tax man, why not take a different approach? What would life be like if we did not fear taxes but instead embraced them? What if we turned the tables on the IRS and made the tax law work for us instead of against us?

Judge Learned Hand once said that "In America, there are two tax systems: one for the informed and one for the uninformed. Both are legal." He is exactly right: The U.S. tax system does have different results for different taxpayers. The truth is that tax law is not designed to be fair. This may be hard to believe, but even two taxpayers who make the same amount of income may pay very different amounts in taxes. Don't believe us? Let's take Bill and Allen, for example.

Bill makes $95,000 of income from his full-time job as an engineer. His only deduction is the standard deduction that the government allows each year. Between federal income taxes, state income taxes, and payroll taxes, he is paying up to 40 percent in taxes.

His friend Allen, on the other hand, makes $95,000 of rental income from his various properties. As you may have guessed, the tax code is filled with perks and loopholes that Allen can take advantage of. He can write off his business-related car expenses, home office expenses, business travel and meals, and depreciation expense, to name a few. After all is said and done, Allen pays zero federal income taxes, zero state income taxes, and zero payroll taxes.

Both taxpayers make $95,000. One pays 40 percent in taxes and the other one pays no taxes at all. Does this seem fair? Of course not. As we have said before, the tax law is not intended to be fair. Instead, it is designed to elicit certain behaviors by providing tax benefits for those behaviors. Knowing that the United States tax system is not fair, we as taxpayers have a decision to make: Who do we want to be? Bill or Allen? Do we want to lose close to half of our hard-earned money to taxes every single year? Or do we want to use the tax code to our advantage and start to shift our behavior to help reduce our tax burden every year?

You may be thinking: *Who doesn't want to be like Allen? Being able to live off of rental income without needing to work, and paying no taxes in the meantime? As ideal as that seems, I just don't know how that can ever apply to my situation.*

If real estate is one of your investment vehicles, it is possible to achieve optimal tax savings with proper planning. Anyone has the ability to change their tax profile, but as with many things in life, it often takes time to change. You may not be able to go from paying 50 percent taxes to paying no taxes immediately this year. In fact, for the vast majority of you reading this book, your tax bill may not be completely eliminated this year. However, with proper planning, you do have the ability to reach optimal tax savings in the long run.

There is a saying that someone is sitting in the shade today because someone planted a tree many years ago. The same can be applied toward taxes. We should take the time now to empower ourselves with the tax-savings tools that are available to us. Taxes saved means more money that we can use to invest and grow our wealth in tax-efficient investments. With the tax-efficient income we generate, we can invest in more real estate and generate more tax-efficient income. Before long, we may be in a position to make taxes work for us instead of us working to pay our taxes.

As we mentioned before, anyone can change their tax profile and start to reduce their taxes. To demonstrate that, let's see how someone like Bill can apply this concept to help reduce his own taxes.

From Lazy Assets to Tax-Saving Investments

Year after year, Bill would always over-withhold on his paychecks. He simply loved the idea of the IRS sending him a refund check every year. To Bill, the larger the refund check, the better he felt he did on his tax filing. When we met Bill for the first time, we told him that getting a large refund was not the best tax strategy. In fact, it was a terrible idea and not a strategy at all! Just because Bill overpaid and received a refund did not mean that Bill reduced his taxes. What it meant is that he made an interest-free loan to the IRS.

Last year, Bill received a $20,000 refund once his taxes were filed. In our first meeting with Bill, we told him that his $20,000 refund was what we consider to be a "lazy asset." In other words, it did not generate any returns. With our advice, Bill decided to reduce his paycheck withholdings. As a result, he had more cash on hand each month. Instead of giving an interest-free loan to the IRS, Bill kept that $20,000 during the year and utilized it as a down payment and bought a $100,000 rental property. By putting that $20,000 lazy asset to work, Bill made $8,500 of rental income that he otherwise would not have earned if he had continued to prepay his taxes to the IRS.

As an investor, Bill was on a new path toward tax savings. He was able to take full advantage of the loopholes in the tax code that he was not otherwise able to utilize before. He could reduce his taxes with legitimate business write-offs such as car, travel, meals, home office, and depreciation. With the right tax plan in place, Bill was able to wipe out the taxes on the $8,500 of his rental income. He could keep the entire $8,500 that he made without paying part of it to the IRS this year.

With some additional planning using some of the strategies we cover in this book, we were also able to help Bill supersize his write-offs where an additional loss of $20,000 was created. These losses were then utilized to offset Bill's taxes from his W-2 income. At a federal and state income tax rate of just under 40 percent, the $20,000 additional loss could save Bill another $8,000 in taxes.

By shifting his tax dollars to real estate investments, this small change resulted in $16,500 of additional cash in his pocket. What could Bill do with that additional cash? Well, maybe he could consider utilizing that as a down payment to purchase another $100,000 rental property to create even more tax-efficient income.

At first glance, it may have seemed impossible for Bill to take advantage of the tax code. As a full-time employee with no investments, Bill appeared to be out of luck. But with even such a small shift, Bill was starting to utilize the tax code to his advantage. If Bill is able to replicate this strategy year after year, it may not be long before he can have enough rental income to replace his earnings from his job. He may then be in a position to live tax efficiently, just like his friend Allen.

As you can see, the tax code can be cracked. It can be utilized to work for you instead of working against you. Is it easy to crack the tax code? Unfortunately, the answer is no. Just as the tax code is filled with loopholes that can save you lots in taxes, it is also filled with land mines and pitfalls that can trap your tax dollars. Can it be done by the average real estate investor? Absolutely.

To crack the tax code and have it work for your benefit, there are a few initial points that you should understand:

#1: Don't Be Afraid

Yes, taxes can be intimidating. Let's face it, with the tax code being over 2,600 pages and thousands more in regulations, court cases, and rulings, it is nearly impossible for anyone to claim they are an *expert* on all things taxes.

If you have no financial background, taxes may seem like a completely foreign language. The first step to cracking the tax code is to understand that you will not know everything there is to know about taxes. No one does. Not even the most renowned CPAs in the country. The good news, though, is that the majority of what is in the tax law probably has no impact on your situation. You don't need to worry about understanding farming taxation or manufacturing rules. If you are a real estate investor, only a few sections of the tax law may apply to you, and as long as you have a basic understanding of those sections, you are ahead of the game.

#2: Know the Basics

Although you don't need to know all things tax-related in order to crack the tax code, you do need to have a general understanding of tax law to have taxes work for you. You should, for example, learn some of the tax sections that provide benefits specifically for investors. Knowing some of the real estate–specific tax benefits—such as depreciation, tax-deferred exchanges, real estate professional status, and self-directed investing—can be significant to you as an investor.

We're not saying that you need to know all the depreciation rules and regulations. You don't necessarily need to know how to calculate depreciation or even how many years to depreciate every single asset. Knowing the basics simply means that you should generally understand how depreciation works, and more important, how depreciation can help you reduce taxes.

The goal here is not for you to become a CPA or to teach others tax strategies. Rather, you need to know enough that you can ask your tax advisor the right questions.

#3: Know When to Ask Questions

If cracking the tax code starts by empowering yourself with a basic understanding of relevant tax benefits, then the next action item is to make sure you have a team of tax experts who can help you take advantage of those tax benefits. They can also help keep you updated on the latest strategies that are available as tax law changes. One of the reasons no one can claim to be an expert in all things taxes is the constant change. Many people are excited to hear of highly publicized changes such as tax reform or tax overhaul, but in reality, tax law changes throughout the year. In fact, on any given day, a tax court can make a decision that alters or redefines the way a law should be interpreted. Those little-known changes can be just as impactful as those that are highly publicized in the national media.

Many investors like to search online for tax-saving solutions. Type in "tax strategies for real estate investors" and you'll come across hundreds of thousands of articles on this topic. Be careful if you are thinking of implementing a strategy by yourself that you learn online. Tax planning is not a do-it-yourself activity. A strategy that worked for your neighbor could end up being worthless to you if you miss any of the underlying details.

Does this mean that, as an investor, you need to sign up for news updates on tax changes? Of course not. However, it does mean that if real estate is one of your main wealth-building vehicles, your tax advisor should be someone who specializes in the real estate arena and is up-to-date on the latest tax changes with respect to real estate. Your job is simply to ask the right questions and leverage the expertise of your tax advisors.

When we talk about asking questions, we don't just mean *you* should be the one asking questions. Your tax advisor should be asking you questions as well. For example, when you discuss purchasing a property, your tax advisor should be asking you, How do you plan to finance the property? How much do you expect to earn from this property? Will there be other partners involved? How long do you plan to hold on to the property? And what will be your exit strategy for this property? The answers to these questions will help your tax advisor develop a tax-saving plan for you.

#4: Plan Ahead

As you may have guessed, tax savings don't just happen by chance. They happen by design with careful and continuous planning. The next step to cracking the tax code is to plan ahead.

There is a major difference between tax planning and tax preparation. Tax preparation is simply reporting to the IRS what you did last year. If all you wanted to do was pay your taxes and be done with it, you could easily utilize a free online tax software. Tax preparation is when you sit in front of your tax preparer in April and tell them for the first time that you sold a property last year for a large gain. You hope they may have a strategy to help you reduce taxes, but they tell you it's too late. They simply enter in all the income and expenses you provide for last year and give you the bad news of how much you need now to pay the IRS.

You are reading this book because you want more than that. You want to be proactive in reducing your taxes. You are looking for a tax strategist to plan ahead with you during the year to see what can be done now to reduce your taxes in the future. You want a tax advisor to walk you through what is tax deductible and what is not. For the items that may or may not be deductible, you want to know what *can* be done to turn them into legitimate business expenses. The truth is that there are tax deductions everywhere; you just need to know how to take advantage of them legally.

Many people have the misconception that tax planning is for the super wealthy. That unless you have millions of dollars in income or assets, tax planning is a waste of time and money. It may surprise you that tax planning often has nothing to do with how much money you make. For example, we had a client who had no income and a lot of tax losses after claiming depreciation and write-offs on their rentals. Although they had no income in that year to reduce taxes, one strategy we implemented was to utilize their tax losses to convert a large chunk of their taxable retirement money into tax-free Roth money. Instead of wasting the tax losses, we helped them take full advantage of the losses by moving money from a taxable bucket into a permanently tax-free bucket for them. How would you like to have tax-free money for the rest of your life? Or how would you like to leave tax-free money to your children and grandchildren so they never have to pay taxes on that income?

Although tax planning is not limited to those with very high income, it often does have a lot to do with what "type" of income you make. Fortunately for us, the tax code heavily favors real estate investors. As an investor, you may have heard that there are many wonderful tax perks and loopholes available for us. However, it is important to understand that since the tax law favors real estate investors, it does not mean that your taxes will magically go down because you invest in real estate. You must know how to find the strategies, which strategies work in your unique situation, and more important, how to implement them correctly.

#5: Make Tax Savings Part of Your Daily Life

Tax planning does not mean speaking with your tax advisors once during the year and never calling them again until tax time. One of the easiest ways to significantly reduce your taxes is to create systems that will help you to consider taxes as part of your everyday decisions.

For example, when you are purchasing paper and stamps at your local office supply store, ask yourself whether these are items that are ordinary and necessary to you as a real estate investor. If the answer is yes, keep a copy of that receipt and make sure to track that expense as a tax-deductible item. If you are planning a vacation and also planning to look at some investment properties, make sure to speak with your tax advisor before booking your travel plans. This helps to ensure that you maximize your tax write-off on that upcoming trip. As an investor, you should contact your tax advisor before selling any investment properties. If you are selling the properties for a gain, there may be strategies to defer taxes, as well as strategies to offset the taxes. If you are selling for a loss, there may be strategies to help you take the best advantage of those losses to create the largest tax refund.

Making taxes part of your daily life does not mean you have to walk around thinking about taxes all day long. All it takes is a little bit of practice to keep taxes in the back of your mind. Tax planning needs to be done proactively during the year to get the intended results. As indicated previously, tax law changes throughout the year. Your financial situation will likely change throughout the year as well. Tax rates, amounts, limitations, and loopholes are also constantly changing. To keep up to date with the latest tax rates and tax breaks, please visit our site at www.keystonecpa.com to make sure you have access to the latest information.

Whether you are an investor who's been in the industry for decades or a brand-new investor just starting out, the tax code is filled with strategies and loopholes designed to help protect your hard-earned money. If you currently don't have a plan to reduce taxes, then you will likely end up using the plan the IRS has in store for you, which effectively is a plan to pay the most taxes possible. To have an effective tax plan means finding legal ways to minimize your taxes and to protect your assets.

Can the tax code be broken and used to our advantage as real estate investors? Yes. Can we plan proactively to utilize legal tax benefits to control our tax bill? Absolutely. The rest of this book is filled with stories that showcase just how powerful these strategies can be and how to use them correctly to protect your hard-earned money.

CHAPTER 1

TAX REFORM AND THE SAVVY REAL ESTATE INVESTOR

"There may be liberty and justice for all, but there are tax breaks only for some."

—MARTIN A. SULLIVAN

After more than thirty years, the United States has finally enacted one of the most comprehensive tax changes in recent history. Its official name is "The Tax Cuts and Jobs Act of 2017," although we will refer to it simply as "tax reform" in this book. As you may have already guessed, the highly anticipated tax reform left some taxpayers as winners and others as losers. Fortunately, real estate investors clearly fell within the winners' group. You may already know that, historically speaking, real estate investors have enjoyed some of the best tax loopholes within the tax code, but tax reform actually took the tax benefits to a whole new level. From larger deductions to tax-free income, it has never been more tax efficient to be a real estate investor than it is today. In fact, there is a brand-new tax break called the Opportunity Zone to which we have dedicated an entire chapter later in the book.

Many of the changes can drastically slash your taxes. When implemented correctly, some of the new benefits can even create generational wealth. However, as we said earlier, there were some losers from the tax reform changes as well, and some of those do apply to real estate. There are strategies to get around those new limitations, too. In this chapter, we will go over some of the most important tax reform changes that impact investors, as well as ways to avoid the new tax traps.

Mortgage Interest

One of the highly publicized tax reform changes that critics often discuss is the new limitation on primary home mortgage interest. Under tax reform, if you purchase a new primary home, your mortgage interest deduction is now limited to $750,000 of debt. This means that if your home has a $1 million loan, you can only deduct interest on the first $750,000 of loan. The interest on the remaining $250,000 of loan becomes non-deductible. This was a negative tax change because prior to tax reform, you could deduct interest on primary home loans up to $1 million.

Let's take Cindy, for example. Cindy owns a primary home with a $1 million loan on which she pays $40,000 of interest. In 2017, she was able to deduct the entire $40,000 of interest. Cindy sells her home in 2018 and purchases a new home where she also has a $1 million loan. She pays $40,000 of interest during the year on the new home. Under tax reform Cindy is only able to write off the interest on the first $750,000 of debt, which is 75 percent. As such, her home mortgage interest deduction in 2018 is now reduced to $30,000 (75 percent of the original $40,000).

There are a few key items to note on the primary home mortgage interest changes. First, the limitations only apply to new homes that are purchased, and they do not apply to homes that were purchased prior to tax reform. For example, if Cindy did not sell her old primary home, she would still be able to continue deducting all of her mortgage interest on that home up to $1 million of debt.

Now, what if Cindy decides to keep the home but refinances the loan in order to get a lower interest rate? Even if she refinances her home loan, she would be able to continue to deduct interest on the original $1 million loan. The only difference is that interest deduction on a refinance may be reduced if the balance on that loan is lower than $1 million. For example, if Cindy pays down the loan, and it has an outstanding balance of $950,000 at the time of the refinance, her interest deduction would be limited to $950,000 worth of debt. Alternatively, if she refinances her $1 million loan and it becomes a $1,200,000 loan because she took out some equity from her home, then her interest deduction would still be limited to her original $1 million loan balance. That means the interest paid on the new $200,000 portion of her home loan would not be deductible.

Another change under tax reform was that home equity lines of credit (HELOCs) on primary homes are no longer deductible. Before tax reform, you were able to deduct HELOC interest of up to $100,000. After tax reform, there are generally no tax deductions for lines of credit on primary homes. Note, though, that this change only applies to primary homes.

Interest Tracing

One important thing to keep in mind is that the new mortgage interest limitations only apply to primary homes, not investment properties. This means that for your rental properties, your interest is generally still going to be fully deductible, regardless of the loan amount. If you own an apartment building that has a loan of $5 million, all that interest can still be fully tax-deductible. HELOCs on investment properties also remain fully tax-deductible.

With that in mind, even though there is a new limitation on primary home mortgage interest, there are ways to overcome that limitation using interest tracing. In interest tracing, the IRS allows you to look at how the loan proceeds are used in order to determine if and how the related interest can be deductible. For example, if you took out a HELOC on your primary home but used the loan proceeds to purchase rental properties, you can turn that interest from being non-deductible to deductible interest. Let's go over an example.

Ethan wants to get into real estate investing. He doesn't have a lot of cash on hand to invest, but he does have quite a bit of equity in his primary home. Ethan decides to take cash out using a home equity line of credit of $200,000 and use that to buy a rental property. Although interest on a HELOC on your primary residence is now non-deductible under tax reform, Ethan is still able to deduct the interest on his $200,000 of HELOC because the $200,000 was used to purchase a rental property.

How does the IRS know what the $200,000 is used for? The best way to audit-proof yourself for interest tracing is to use a separate bank account. Let's assume that your new rental property will be held in an LLC. You would take the $200,000 loan out of your primary home, and the loan proceeds will first go into your personal account. You would then move that money from your personal account into the rental LLC account. From that LLC account, you can then use your money to purchase the new rental property. This way, if you are ever audited, you would be able to show the IRS that this money was moved into the LLC account to be used for investment purposes. If you do not plan to own your rental in an LLC, it might make sense to open a separate personal account and simply designate that account to only be used specifically for rental activities. This way, you can move the loan proceeds into that separate account.

Accelerated Depreciation

One of the biggest positive changes under tax reform is the 100 percent bonus depreciation. Under the new bonus depreciation rules, you can immediately write off certain assets in the first year instead of depreciating them over multiple years.

As an example, let's continue with Ethan's scenario above. Let's assume that Ethan uses $200,000 to purchase a $500,000 rental duplex. He plans to rent out the property as a furnished home to visiting physicians at the local hospital. Ethan spends $25,000 to purchase furniture, appliances, bedding, and other items to get the duplex ready. Due to tax reform, Ethan does not need to wait to depreciate the cost of these assets over multiple years. Instead, Ethan can write off the entire $25,000 of purchases this year using bonus depreciation. If we assume that Ethan is in a combined federal and state tax bracket of 45 percent, then he can save more than $11,000 in taxes this year. Plus, bonus depreciation can now apply to both new and used items alike—so if Ethan decided to buy used furniture to save some money, the used furniture is still eligible for 100 percent bonus depreciation.

In addition to furniture and fixtures, bonus depreciation can be applied to many other assets. If you purchased a computer to manage your investing activities, that computer is eligible. If you worked from a home office to manage your rental properties, the furniture you buy for that home office is also eligible. What if you used your car for your real estate activities? Well, that car may be eligible for bonus depreciation, as well. If you purchased an eligible vehicle for $40,000 that you use in your real estate business, that could be a $40,000 tax deduction all in just one year.

The other great thing about bonus depreciation is that it is available to financed assets as well—if you purchased a $40,000 truck with financing, your tax deduction could be as high as $40,000, even if you financed the entire purchase. Using a combined 45 percent federal and state tax rate, you could be saving around $18,000 using this strategy, even if you paid nothing out of pocket this year.

Although bonus depreciation applies to many different types of assets that an investor may purchase, it does not apply to the rental property itself. Ethan can't write off the $500,000 purchase price of the rental property; the rental property building must still be depreciated over multiple years. There are, however, ways to combine bonus depreciation with a cost segregation strategy to accelerate the depreciation of the building, which we will discuss in Chapter 2.

Section 179 Expensing

In addition to bonus depreciation, another tool to accelerate your tax deductions as an investor is the new and improved Section 179 expensing. Similar to bonus depreciation, Section 179 allows you to take an immediate tax write-off, rather than wait to depreciate an item over multiple years. Under this improved tax benefit, you may be able to expense up to $1 million of assets related to your investment properties in the first year. If you are an investor involved in commercial properties, the new law allows you to take an immediate write-off of money spent on roofs, HVAC equipment, alarm systems, fire protection, and security systems.

Meals and Entertainment

A new limitation that came out as part of tax reform is related to entertainment expenses. Under tax reform, entertainment expenses are no longer tax-deductible. In the past, if you took an investor out to a show for entertainment purposes, it used to be a legitimate expense. After tax reform, however, even if the entertainment occurred for business purposes, it is no longer deductible as a business expense.

Because the IRS took away business entertainment deductions, many people were under the wrong assumption that business meals were taken away as well. The truth is that business meals remain tax-deductible for all investors. If you went to a local real estate meeting and had dinner before or after that meeting, that meal is still tax-deductible. If you traveled out of town to look at rental properties, that meal remains tax-deductible. Essentially, tax deductions for meals have remained pretty much the same after tax reform. If you are someone who does need to entertain quite a bit for your real estate business, you probably already know that, more often than not, meals are part of your entertainment. For example, if you wanted to schmooze with some potential investors and take them to a baseball game, odds are that you will have some food and drinks at the game. In that scenario, although the baseball tickets are no longer tax-deductible, the hot dog and beer are still legitimate tax deductions. As long as the costs of the meals can be separated out from the entertainment, meal costs that occur during a business entertainment event can still be written off for tax purposes. If you are taking clients to dinner and a show, make sure to split out your costs of the dinner from the show so that you can maximize your meal deductions.

Pass-Through Tax Deduction

Can you think of anything better than larger tax deductions? If tax-free income is what you were thinking about, then your wish may now be a reality. For the first time in history, the IRS has now created a brand-new benefit under tax reform to allow some tax-free income to real estate investors. The new tax break is often referred to as the pass-through tax deduction.

In the pass-through tax deduction, the first 20 percent of certain types of income may be completely tax-free. For example, if you are a landlord with taxable rental income of $100, the first $20 of that may be completely tax-free, and you only pay taxes on the remaining $80. Even better, pass-through tax deduction is available to almost all types of real estate income.

First, let's clarify some of the myths about this new tax benefit. Because it is most commonly referred to as a pass-through tax deduction, many investors are under the wrong impression that in order to receive the 20 percent tax-free treatment, your real estate must be held inside of a pass-through entity. That is actually incorrect. The pass-through tax deduction has nothing to do with legal entities. This means that whether you operate your real estate business through an LLC, S corporation, partnership, or simply in your personal name, it does not impact your ability to claim this benefit at all.

So how exactly do we know what type of income is eligible for this 20 percent tax-free treatment? First, let's take a look at what the IRS has defined as income that is *not* eligible: W-2 income, interest income, dividends and capital gains income, and retirement distributions income. So if your real estate income is not from one of these listed categories, there is a good chance that you may benefit from the 20 percent tax break.

Let's dive into how the 20 percent tax-free benefit can impact the most common ways that investors make money in real estate.

House Flipping

Commonly referred to as fix-and-flip, house flipping is when you purchase a property to rehab and resell, which can create a lot of profit in a short amount of time. One of the issues with house flipping, though, is the high taxes associated with flips. When compared to rental properties, investors who flip houses often end up paying higher taxes. However, under tax reform, flip profit is eligible for the 20 percent tax-free treatment.

Let's take an example: Miles lives in Florida and recently got into the flipping business. Last year, Miles made a little over $100,000 of profit by flipping four properties. Normally, Miles would need to pay taxes on his $100,000 income. However, since flip profit is eligible for the pass-through tax deduction, the first 20 percent of Miles's flip profit is tax-free. For Miles, this means that the first $20,000 of his flip income would be at zero tax. Assuming that he's in the 24 percent tax bracket, this new tax break saves him up to $4,800 in federal income taxes this year.

As we mentioned previously, eligibility for the pass-through entity tax break is based on the type of income rather than legal entities. Since profit from flipping houses is eligible income, Miles would receive this tax benefit regardless of whether he operated his house-flipping business in an LLC, S corporation, partnership, or a sole proprietorship.

Wholesale Income

Unlike house flipping, a wholesaling investor does not intend to purchase or rehab the property. Instead, the wholesaler negotiates the purchase of a property from the seller, then sells the property to another buyer for a higher price than what the property is listed for on the contract. This income is commonly referred to as wholesale fees.

From a tax perspective, wholesale income is treated the same way as flip profit, which means that it can also be subject to higher taxes as compared to rental income. However, similar to flip profit, wholesale income is also eligible for the pass-through tax break—meaning that if you made $100,000 in wholesale fees, up to 20 percent of that can be completely tax-free under tax reform.

Real Estate Commissions

Another way to make money in real estate is to earn commissions. Whether they are commissions on your own properties or from helping others buy and sell properties, commissions can create a significant amount of income for many investors. From a tax perspective, there are a few different ways that commissions income may be earned:

- If you own a brokerage firm, the income you earn from your clients would generally be eligible for the pass-through tax deduction.
- As an agent, one way to earn commissions income is to earn it as a 1099 contractor. This commonly occurs if you are a Realtor working as an agent under a broker. You may get a commission split on any deals you are involved in, and the broker may issue you a 1099 for your share of that profit. In that scenario, your commissions income would generally be eligible for the pass-through tax break as well.
- If you are working as a real estate agent under a broker, your commissions can be paid as a W-2 from the broker rather than as a 1099 contractor. If your income is earned as a W-2, that income generally will not be eligible for the pass-through tax deduction. The IRS specifically states that W-2 income is not eligible for the pass-through tax break. As you can see, this can be a tax trap for the unwary. Although the underlying income is commissions from the sale of real estate, it is not eligible for the tax break if that income is paid to you as W-2 income. As such, if you are able to earn your income as a 1099 contractor instead, you may get significantly more tax savings as compared to a W-2 Realtor.

Note Investors

We discussed previously that having a legal entity (an LLC, S-Corporation, or Partnership) is not a requirement in order to benefit from this pass-through tax deduction. It is also important to note that simply having a legal entity does not automatically ensure that the income earned in the entity is eligible for the 20 percent tax benefit, either. Ultimately, it is the *type* of income that determines whether it is eligible for the tax-free treatment. Let's go over an example:

Jean has been a real estate investor for as long as she can remember. She bought her first rental property in her early twenties and has grown her portfolio from a few single-family homes to now owning a few apartment buildings. Jean has now retired and wants to spend her time traveling to visit her kids and grandkids. To cut down on her property management time, Jean decides to sell all her single-family homes and keep only the apartments that have on-site managers. Jean needs a place to invest the cash that she obtained from the sale of her rentals.

Because real estate is Jean's preferred investment vehicle, she makes the decision to use her money to invest in real estate notes. With the proceeds from the sale of her rentals, Jean invests as a private lender and loans her money to a few local investors who flipped properties. As a private lender, Jean earns interest income of $25,000 that year.

Unfortunately for Jean, interest income from a note investment is not eligible for the pass-through tax deduction. As such, Jean would need to pay taxes on the entire $25,000 of interest she earned because the IRS has indicated that interest income is not eligible for this particular tax benefit. This is the case even if Jean were to put her money in an LLC and then have the LLC lend out to flippers. The reason is because in both scenarios, Jean is generating interest income.

Luckily, with some strategic planning, Jean may be able to make the tax law work in her favor. What if instead of lending to the flip project, Jean became a partner in the flip project? In that scenario, Jean's income is switched from interest income to flip profit, which may then allow Jean to receive the benefits of the pass-through tax deduction. With some minor structuring changes, Jean may be able to receive the tax benefits of the pass-through tax break after all.

Management Income

Whether you earn property management income from your own rentals or from managing properties for other investors, both may be eligible for the 20 percent tax-free treatment. If you are a syndicator who has put together an investment fund to pool investor money, you may also be receiving asset management fees to help manage the fund. In addition, you may be earning acquisition fees, as well as disposition fees, for your role in putting together the deal. All these various types of active income may be eligible for the pass-through tax deduction, which can be extremely impactful.

Here's another example: William was a syndication client of ours who put two commercial deals together last year. As the active manager of the syndication, William earned a little over $200,000 last year in acquisition fees and asset management fees. Because of the flow-through tax deduction under tax reform, $40,000 of William's income was completely tax-free last year. William received this benefit simply because the income he earned was eligible income under tax reform. There were no additional action items William needed to do to receive this benefit; it was just a nice little gift from the government.

Rental Income

Does rental income qualify for this wonderful 20 percent tax-free treatment? Unfortunately, the answer is not a simple yes or no. As with many things in the tax world, the answer to this question is "It depends." Although you can see that most types of real estate-related income are eligible for this tax break, the IRS didn't make the tax break available to all rental income. Essentially, the tax break is available for rental income when it is considered a "trade or business."

When is a rental property considered a "trade or business" that is eligible for this 20 percent tax-free treatment? This is an extremely subjective test. Generally speaking, your rental could be considered a trade or business if you were very actively involved in the day-to-day operations of the property. In other words, your work in the rental property goes beyond the normal activities that an investor would typically do. Does that mean you must manage your own properties? Do you do your own repairs? Are you on call for the tenants? Again, this is a very subjective test to meet. The best way to look at this requirement is that the more tasks you perform to be actively involved with your rentals, the better your chances are of being eligible for this tax break.

Since the "trade or business" requirement is a difficult one to define, the IRS provided a safe-harbor test to help you determine whether your rental income is eligible for this pass-through tax break. Chances are high if you meet all four of the following requirements:

- You need to have separate books and records for your rental real estate activities.
- There needs to be over 250 hours of rental service activities done for the year.

- You must be able to produce records and documents to prove these hours and services actually occurred.
- You need to attach a signed statement to the tax return to indicate the safe harbor requirement has been met.

Let's go over these requirements in more detail.

SEPARATE BOOKS AND RECORDS

The requirement for separate books and records for your rental real estate activities means that you should have a ledger that tracks the income and expenses of each rental property. For example, let's assume that Hannah owns two rental properties in her personal name, but she has a separate bank account for them. She keeps a spreadsheet that records all of the income and expenses of each property. In this case, Hannah's spreadsheet is sufficient to satisfy the separate books and records requirement. Similarly, had Hannah utilized a bookkeeping software that maintains all of this information, that would satisfy this requirement as well.

What if Hannah used her personal bank for all rental-related activities? And what if Hannah did not have Excel or bookkeeping software for her two properties but she simply used her bank account statements as her accounting records? In either case, Hannah would not satisfy this requirement because bank statements are not the same as books and records.

250 HOURS OF SERVICES

The second requirement is that at least 250 hours of rental services were performed for your rental properties during the year. Here is a list of services that qualify for the 250-hour test:
- Marketing the property for rent
- Negotiating and signing leases
- Reviewing tenant applications
- Collecting rent
- Managing the property
- Dealing in the daily operations, maintenance, and repair of the property
- Purchasing materials
- Supervising employees and contractors for the property

As you can see, this list includes most of the day-to-day activities that you may be involved in with your properties. The added benefit is that the 250-hour requirement does not need to come from tasks that are only performed by you as the investor. In fact, these tasks can be performed by your employees, agents, and contractors as well. If you hired a property manager and they spent at least 250 hours doing these tasks for you, you would meet the 250-hour safe harbor requirement.

In addition, the 250 hours of rental activities may be combined across your rental properties. This means that, in Hannah's example, she does not need to spend 250 hours on each of her two rentals. She can combine her properties so that if she spends at least 250 hours in both of her rentals together, she could meet the hours' requirement.

There are, however, activities that do not count toward the 250-hour requirement, such as the following:

- Property acquisition
- Financing
- Studying reports on operations
- Planning, managing, or construction of property improvements
- Hours spent traveling to and from properties

DOCUMENTATION

The third safe harbor requirement is that you must have records and documents to support the 250 hours of time that was spent. The timekeeping record can include time reports, logs, or other similar documents. That record should include a description of the service that was done, the date the service took place, the number of hours it took, who performed the service, and which property it related to. One of the requirements is that the records and documents must be contemporaneous—they must be kept throughout the year and not just done at the end of the year or at the time of an audit. If an IRS agent were auditing you and requested your time log, you cannot ask them to give you a month to put your log together. The log must have been kept and updated throughout the year.

SIGNED STATEMENT

The last requirement under the safe harbor test is the easiest to meet. To claim the safe harbor and be able to have your rental properties qualify for the 20 percent tax break, you simply need to sign a statement and attach it to your tax return indicating to the IRS that you meet the safe harbor requirements. Keep in mind that this is a separate statement you would create to attach to the tax return. It is neither a specific tax form to fill out nor a special box to check. A sample of a safe harbor statement can be found in Appendix A.

EXCEPTIONS

Although most rental income can be eligible for the 20 percent tax break, the IRS has listed two types of rental income that would not receive this benefit. The first one is income from triple net lease properties. If you earn rental income from a triple net investment, that would not be eligible for the 20 percent tax break. The second type of rental income that is not eligible for the tax break is rental income generated from a property that is also used as your home during the year. If you rent out one of the rooms in your home, the rental income from that room would not qualify for this tax break. In another example, if you moved out of your home and turned it into a rental during the year, the income from that property would also not be eligible for the tax break this year.

Buy, Rehab, Rent, Refinance, and Repeat (BRRRR) Properties

Do investors using the BRRRR strategy receive the 20 percent tax break? The BRRRR method is used when an investor purchases a property, does some rehab to improve the property, rents the property out to a tenant, and then refinances to cash their equity out of the property. From a tax perspective, a BRRRR property is just like any other rental property you own. It is treated the same as a regular buy and hold transaction. If your regular rental income meets the eligibility requirements for the 20 percent tax break, your BRRRR properties should receive that benefit also.

Short-Term Rentals

Over the past few years, there has been a steady increase in the number of short-term vacation rentals on the market. Many investors are finding that turning their long-term rentals into short-term rentals can potentially generate much higher cash flow. From a tax perspective, there are two potential tax treatments when it comes to short-term rental income:

- The first scenario is when hotel-type services are provided to the guests. Common examples of hotel-type services include room service, food and beverage, daily cleaning, and maybe hotel transportation. If your short-term rental operates similar to a hotel business, that rental income would generally be eligible for the 20 percent pass-through tax break.

- If you are a short-term rental investor and you do not provide any hotel type services, then the income from your short-term rentals is treated exactly the same way as the income from regular long-term rentals. In this scenario, whether that short-term rental income is eligible for the 20 percent tax-break will just depend again on whether your regular rental income would qualify.

Syndication Investments

Real estate syndication is a way for several investors to pool their money to invest in a large deal. In a syndication investment, the property is typically held in a legal entity such as an LLC. As an investor, you will invest your money in exchange for a partial ownership of that LLC. As an owner of that LLC, you will earn income based on your share of profit that is generated in that LLC.

Whether your investment in the syndication will be eligible for the 20 percent tax break will depend on the type of income the LLC will be earning. For example, if you invested in a syndication that builds and develops homes, it generally will be eligible for this tax break. If you invested in a syndication that holds an apartment building, your income may be eligible for this tax break if it qualifies either as a trade or business or under the safe harbor rules. If you invested in a syndication that made loans to other investors and generates interest income, your share of the interest income is still generally not eligible for that tax break. Of course, before making an investment in a syndication, make sure to speak with your tax advisor so you know whether it will receive the 20 percent tax break.

Different Income, Different Treatment

Oftentimes an investor may make money from several different types of income in any given year. For example, you may be a house flipper who also earned rental income from the properties you decided to hold on to. Or you may be a landlord who also lends money to other investors to earn some interest income. Whether or not your income is eligible for the 20 percent pass-through tax break is determined based on each individual type of income. As an investor, you will see that some of your income may be eligible, while other investment income may not be eligible.

Let's say John works part-time as a salesperson earning W-2 income. He has four rental properties in downtown that he self-manages. John has saved up a little bit of cash, and instead of leaving that in the bank, he loans that money to another investor he knows very well.

Which part of John's income qualifies for the 20 percent tax break? His W-2 income from work and the interest income from his note investment are not eligible for the tax break. However, John's rental income might still be eligible, provided that he can qualify for the safe harbor requirements or can substantiate that his rentals meet the definition of a trade or business.

WHAT DOES IT ALL MEAN?

Real estate investing has become an even better tax shelter with the passage of tax reform. Although new tax limitations have been put on homeowners, none of those restrictions apply to investment properties. In addition, you can often overcome home deduction restrictions when you plan proactively on ways to shift those write-offs toward your investment properties.

With the passage of tax reform, a brand-new 20 percent tax break was created. For many types of real estate income, up to the first 20 percent may be completely tax-free. Common examples of eligible income can include flip income, wholesale income, commissions income, and certain rental income. Real estate income that is not eligible for this tax break includes interest income from note investments and capital gains income.

From an investor's perspective, the vast majority of tax reform changes are designed to help reduce our overall taxes. This is an exciting time to take advantage of tax benefits as a real estate investor, and since tax changes can happen at any time, a benefit that is available today may not be around next year. Make sure to structure your real estate proactively to take advantage of the tax benefits before they expire.

CHAPTER 2

THE DO'S AND DON'TS OF ACCELERATED DEPRECIATION

"Never put off till tomorrow what may be done day after tomorrow just as well."

—**MARK TWAIN**

Meghan has been working at Dot-Tech as a software engineer for close to eight years. In fact, she was one of the first ten employees to join the company. Over the past eight years, the company has grown from a start-up firm with fewer than a dozen employees to a now-recognizable household brand with close to 100 employees and five different offices across the United States. As one of the key employees in the company, Meghan often spends many overtime hours at work. Thankfully, her husband James has a more flexible job as a marketing consultant, so he is able to help out quite a bit at home and with the kids when needed.

To help retain its employees, Dot-Tech has been issuing restricted stock units (RSUs) over the past several years. Previously, none of the restricted stock units really had had an effect on Meghan's taxes in any way, but this will be the year that a large chunk of Meghan's restricted stock units will vest. Meghan doesn't know too much about how RSUs will impact her taxes, but she has heard horror stories from some of her friends in the tech space who had received RSUs in the past. Her friend Rachel said that when the stocks vested, she ended up paying over 45 percent taxes on the fair market value of those stocks.

Meghan and James do not want to lose close to half of their windfall to taxes; instead, they want to get into real estate investing with this money. James's parents were successful real estate investors. Growing up, James and his siblings were able to spend a lot of time with their parents, who had the flexibility and financial freedom to do so. Now that they have grandkids, James's parents have been able to set aside some money for the grandkids' future college education. These financial benefits were the fruits of their labor from many years as real estate investors.

Because they knew the freedom and financial security that can be achieved with real estate investing, Meghan and James made the decision to use her RSUs from work to kick-start their investing venture. With the success of Dot-Tech, it looks like the fair market value of Meghan's restricted stock units will be close to $500,000. That's a good chunk of money to get them well on their way to real estate investing.

However, if Meghan's friend Rachel is correct, then Meghan could lose close to half of the RSU value to taxes. Assuming there will be taxes of 45 percent, the cash that Meghan and James will have after paying taxes on the $500,000 and selling the RSUs will only be $275,000. This just does not sit well with the couple. They know that there has to be a better solution for this. After all, hadn't they heard that there were many tax loopholes for real estate investors? Since they plan on investing in real estate, maybe some of the real estate strategies can help them reduce their upcoming tax bill.

James has always prepared their taxes in the past. Things were simple enough with Meghan's W-2, his sole proprietorship consulting income, and the interest and taxes on their primary home. From time to time, they would make some charitable donations, but other than that, taxes have been fairly straightforward for them. But this year will be different. How will the RSUs be taxed? Will they be able to use their real estate investing plan to reduce the taxes on the RSUs? As much as James wants to tackle this himself and search online for answers, he knows this is too risky a task to take on by himself. He doesn't want to step over a quarter to pick up a nickel.

They decide to do some research and find Mark, a reputable CPA who specializes in working with real estate investors. To their surprise, even though their main concern is the large tax bill on the upcoming RSUs, Mark starts the meeting by asking Meghan and James to elaborate on their overall financial goals and their plans with respect to real estate investing.

Meghan begins by telling Mark that James is expected to make around $100,000 of consulting income this year. Her annual salary will still be the usual $200,000, similar to previous years. Her RSUs will vest this year, and the estimated value of those will be around $500,000. Their plan, if possible, is to sell the stocks immediately upon vesting and turn them into cash of $500,000. They will then use that money to purchase a rental duplex for $500,000. Because James is self-employed, he will then reduce his consulting time and focus solely on real estate in order to qualify as a real estate professional for tax purposes. Although they do not need the cash flow from the rental for living expenses, they want to use real estate to build cash flow and for appreciation so that they could be financially free—just as James's parents were. The only problem, Meghan says, is that it looks like they will first need to pay $225,000 in taxes and can only use the remaining money to start their real estate investing venture.

Mark leans back in his chair, and a big grin appears on his face. According to Mark, it is possible to protect some of the RSU income from taxes. It is also possible to use rental real estate to create cash flow without paying a ton in taxes on the rental income. These goals could be accomplished with the following steps:
1. Sell the RSUs once they vest.
2. Use the cash from the RSUs as a down payment on rental properties.
3. Use leverage from banks, in addition to the down payment, to purchase rental real estate.
4. Maximize rental expenses to offset rental income.
5. Use accelerated depreciation to create a large tax loss.

Mark explains how the RSUs will impact Meghan and James's taxes. First, restricted stock units are taxable as part of W-2 wages in the year of vesting. The amount in taxable income is generally the fair market value of the stock at the time of vesting. As such, since the fair market value of Meghan's RSUs will be $500,000 at the time of vesting, Meghan's W-2 this year will increase by $500,000. The goal, then, is to use rental properties to reduce taxes on this additional $500,000 of income.

Instead of Meghan and James using the cash from the RSU sale to buy an all-cash property, Mark encourages them to consider using leverage to invest in real estate. Leverage allows them to use borrowed money, purchase more investment properties, and grow their real estate at a faster pace. In this case, leverage means using the traditional route of bank financing—saving up money for a down payment and then getting a loan from the bank to purchase a property. Instead of using all of their funds to purchase a duplex with all cash, it could make more sense to purchase three duplexes for a total of $1,500,000 with just some of their funds as a down payment and taking on a loan for the remainder. Even though this could result in less cash flow, it could also result in higher appreciation to have three properties—rather than getting all their cash tied up in one property.

On the tax side, it makes sense to use leverage to purchase multiple properties instead of buying an all-cash property to maximize tax savings using depreciation.

Common Depreciation Myths Revealed

Depreciation can be an investor's best friend when it comes to tax savings. Depreciation is an annual income tax deduction in which the IRS allows an investor to write off the decrease in the property cost each year. We take a tax deduction on our rental properties when we may not have suffered any actual loss on the property—also commonly referred to as a "paper loss." Depreciation, under the IRS definition, is "a tax deduction that allows a taxpayer to recover the cost of a property over time. It is an annual allowance for the wear and tear, deterioration, or obsolescence of the property."

The IRS dictates the depreciation lives for different types of assets. Residential rental buildings, for example, are generally depreciated over 27.5 years. Land, on the other hand, is not depreciable. For example, if Meghan and James purchased a duplex for $500,000 that was made up of $75,000 of land and $425,000 of building, the depreciation on that rental property would be $15,455 per year. Assuming a federal and state tax rate of 45 percent, this could save them close to $7,000 in taxes each year.

$425,000 ÷ 27.5 years = $15,455 depreciation per year

Mark suggests that Meghan and James consider purchasing not just one property but three duplex rentals because—by using leverage to purchase more rentals—they increase cash flow and appreciation as well as the annual tax savings. If Meghan and James purchase three duplex rentals for a total purchase price of $1,500,000, this can mean tax deductions of $46,365 from depreciation alone.

$15,455 \times 3 = \$46,365$ depreciation each year

An important thing to understand about depreciation is that the amount you write off is not dependent on how much money you put down to purchase the property. Rather, it is based on the purchase price of the property. For example, on a $500,000 property, you take the same depreciation expense whether you put 20 percent down or if you put zero money down. This means that it is possible to use depreciation to get tax write-offs, even if you paid no cash out of pocket. Meghan and James's money could either be used to purchase one property to depreciate or to purchase three properties to depreciate. Same out-of-pocket amount, but a much larger depreciation write-off once leverage is added to the equation.

Another important item to note is that depreciation is available as a write-off regardless of whether the property actually increases or decreases in value. Even if a $500,000 property declined in value at the end of Year One and is now only worth $450,000, you are still able to write off your depreciation based on what you purchased it for.

Everything sounds good so far to Meghan and James. They love the idea of using leverage to purchase more rentals to increase cash flow and for appreciation purposes. With Meghan's high W-2 income, they do not see a problem with obtaining bank financing at low interest rates that will allow them to still cash flow the properties. However, even with leverage and the acquisition of three properties, the estimated depreciation deduction is only roughly $46,000. That hardly puts a dent in the taxes they are projecting of $225,000.

The next step, Mark says, is to use a cost segregation study to accelerate the depreciation expense and use that to reduce their anticipated large tax bill. Meghan and James have heard of the term *cost segregation* but are not too familiar with the concept. Based on the limited information they have read about cost segregation online, it seems to be used for large properties, such as apartment buildings or commercial shopping centers. This is the first time they've been told it might help benefit smaller investors such as themselves. They are eager to hear Mark explain the ins and outs of how this can help them.

What Is Cost Segregation?

Cost segregation is a valuable tax strategy for real estate investors that is designed to accelerate depreciation expense into current years rather than waiting to take it slowly over time. It is important to note that cost segregation does not mean you received any *extra* depreciation; it simply means that you are speeding it up and receiving the tax benefit today rather than waiting to receive it over 27.5 years.

We discussed previously that the IRS has a set of rules with respect to the calculation of depreciation. For residential rental real estate buildings, a rule for length of time (usually called the depreciation period) is typically over 27.5 years. With respect to rental real estate, there are more depreciable assets within the building other than just the building itself. Examples of other commonly found depreciable assets on rentals can include flooring, appliances, roof, cabinets, countertops, fixtures, drywall, plumbing, and HVAC. Each of these assets can have different depreciation periods and most are less than 27.5 years.

In essence, cost segregation is an analysis done to accelerate the depreciation on the building. Rather than depreciating the entire amount as "building" over 27.5 years, cost segregation breaks out the components of that building into smaller assets. Once these components are broken out (for example, cabinets, countertops, appliances), they can result in a larger tax deduction in the current years. The depreciation on items such as sidewalks, parking lots, specialty plumbing and electrical, and carpet can then be accelerated over 5 to 15 years instead of 27.5 years. From a tax perspective, cost segregation can create a faster—hence larger—depreciation write-off today. That's why cost segregation is often referred to as "component depreciation" and "accelerated depreciation."

Believe it or not, cost segregation can significantly increase the tax deduction on a rental property. Depending on the underlying property, it may be possible to create depreciation deductions of up to 20 percent to 40 percent of the purchase price of the real estate. If Meghan and James were to invest in $1,500,000 of rentals and implement a cost segregation study that showed accelerated depreciation to be roughly 35 percent of purchase price, that could mean up to $500,000 of depreciation in the first year. This could completely wipe out the taxes from Meghan's RSUs from work and save them $225,000 in income taxes.

Cost segregation sounds like exactly what Meghan and James are looking for. They both had hoped that real estate investing could help them lower their taxes, but they never expected it to wipe out their entire tax bill from the stock windfall.

Common Questions Regarding Cost Segregation

How is a cost segregation done, and can I do it myself?

We have come across investors who have tried the do-it-yourself (DIY) method when it comes to cost segregation. There are also some off-the-shelf software programs that claim they can be used to calculate cost segregation benefits. So, can an investor perform a cost segregation on their own? Sure. Is it recommended? No.

To do a cost segregation, you would need to carefully examine and apply the IRS depreciation policies on land, land improvements, and various classes of personal depreciable property. There are differences between Section 1245 property and Section 1250 property, to name a few. In addition, the IRS has defined thirteen principal elements of a qualified cost segregation. Those elements are:

1. Preparation by someone experienced and with the expertise
2. Detailed description of the cost segregation methodology
3. Use of appropriate documentation
4. Interviews conducted with appropriate parties
5. Use of a common nomenclature
6. Use of a standard numbering system
7. Explanation of the legal analysis
8. Determination of unit costs and engineering "take-offs"
9. Organization of assets into lists or groups
10. Reconciliation of final allocated costs to total the actual costs
11. Explanation of the treatment of indirect costs
12. Identification and listing of section 1245 property
13. Consideration of a variety of related aspects (for example, sampling techniques, change in accounting)

As you can see, it is more involved than simply breaking out the cost of dishwashers and sinks. Unless you are well versed in the thirteen elements above, we would not recommend taking the DIY approach to a cost segregation; it should be done by a reputable engineering or consulting firm. There is a set of specific rules and guidelines that must be followed in order to break out the components of a building and accurately split out the property for depreciation calculation. Doing it yourself can be complicated, time-consuming, and most of all . . . risky. Our recommendation is to leave this to the professionals and hire a cost segregation firm.

Aren't cost segregation studies very expensive?

This is a concern we have heard from time to time. As with most investment decisions, there is a cost/benefit analysis that should be done in order to determine whether this strategy makes sense for a given investor in a given year. It may work for you but not your investor friend. It may have been a bad strategy for you last year but a great strategy for you this year. It all depends on the facts and circumstances of each case. However, if a 20 percent to 40 percent write-off in the first five years can save you tens to hundreds of thousands of dollars in taxes, then it very well could make sense to incur the cost to get the analysis done.

When is a cost segregation study done?

First, accelerated depreciation can be taken at any time on a rental property you own. It does not need to be taken in the year you first purchase the property, or in the first year the property is placed into service. It doesn't need to be done in Year Two, or Three, or Four . . . you get the idea. Essentially, cost segregation can be done at any time during your rental holding period.

Investors are often under the impression that cost segregation must be done before the end of the tax year. Although most tax strategies do need to be implemented before the end of the year in order to reduce taxes for that year, that rule actually does not apply to cost segregations. In fact, we often recommend that clients wait until the tax return is being prepared before making a decision on whether a cost segregation would make sense for that year. For example, if I am expecting to pay taxes at 37 percent, I may want to get a cost segregation done to reduce my taxes. What if, though, by the time I prepare my actual tax return, it turns out that I actually ended up in the 10 percent bracket? I may want to forgo cost segregation for now and reconsider it as a strategy for a future year.

The best time to decide whether to do a cost segregation is when you know how much in taxes you would actually save. The cost segregation does need to be done before the tax return is filed, however, so you don't want to wait too long to start analyzing its cost/benefits.

Isn't cost segregation only for large properties?

Just like Meghan and James, many investors are under the impression that cost segregation is a strategy to be used only for the heavy hitters of real estate investing. Although it is true that larger apartment buildings and commercial property can benefit greatly from accelerated depreciation, it does not mean that smaller properties or single families would not benefit. Since depreciation is calculated based on the purchase price of the property, price is often more important than the property's size when it comes to cost segregation benefits. For instance, a single-family property purchased for $500,000 may have the same or even better benefits than a ten-unit apartment building purchased for $250,000. Many investors are pleasantly surprised to find that it can make sense to consider cost segregation on smaller properties with a basis of $300,000 and sometimes even less. It can also make sense for an investor who may have three smaller rentals that total $300,000 in depreciable basis as well. It really depends on the property itself, its location, and the profile of the investor. In any case, it is certainly worth at least an analysis to see if the benefit outweighs the cost.

If I do a cost segregation, won't I just pay more in taxes when I sell the property?

This is a common concern from investors who are contemplating a cost segregation. An investor's tax basis is generally what they paid for the property. It is increased by improvements made to the property and decreased by depreciation taken each year on the property. Since a cost segregation accelerates the depreciation of a property, the investor's tax basis is decreased as a result.

Although it is true that a cost segregation decreases the investor's tax basis, which thereby increases the future capital gains on the sale of the property, it still can make sense to do a cost segregation. If I asked you whether you would prefer to pay the IRS taxes today or wait to pay them ten years down the road when you sell the property, which would you choose? Most investors we know would choose to pay later. This is exactly the same concept with respect to cost segregation. You are accelerating the depreciation today to pay less tax today instead of waiting for that benefit until future years.

Another thing to consider is the difference in tax rates. Let's consider Meghan and James's situation: If they use a cost segregation to offset their income in the year where they had large taxable income—on which they would have paid taxes at a 45 percent tax rate—that means tax savings of 45 percent on the accelerated depreciation. In addition, when they sell the property down the road, they will either pay taxes at a lower capital gains rate or on a recapture rate of 25 percent, both of which are lower than the tax savings they receive today of 45 percent. In this example, not only do Meghan and James defer the taxes into future years, they also receive permanent tax savings of at least 20 percent as a result of this strategy.

If I write off $100,000 in depreciation, isn't the IRS sure to audit me?

This is a common fear for investors evaluating cost segregation. Fortunately, that does not appear to be the case. With the large number of investor tax returns we have prepared, a sizable percentage of them include accelerated depreciation. Of those, very few returns have been selected for IRS audit. Of the ones audited, there were only a few cases where the IRS agent actually asked to look into the cost segregation calculation. This is why it is extremely important to make sure you are working with a reputable cost segregation firm and not doing it yourself. In the instances where the IRS inquired about the calculation, the cost segregation firms were able to produce their work papers to document and support their analysis. After that, the auditors signed off on those calculations without any further questions.

Different Person, Different Results

As with everything regarding taxes, this strategy is not a one-size-fits-all solution. Although it works wonders for Meghan and James, it may be a terrible strategy if used incorrectly by another taxpayer.

Edward graduated from dental school and started his career as a dentist. He is making a great living getting paid W-2 income of just over $150,000. He's eager to get into real estate investing. With his high W-2 salary and a nice down payment, Edward is able to purchase two rental properties in his first year as an investor. He attends a lot of local real estate investment clubs and meets many other investors. That is where he learns about the tax benefits of cost segregation. Another investor tells Edward that cost segregation is the best-kept secret in real estate investing and that it had helped her wipe out her tax bill and resulted in a large refund.

After hearing this, Edward gets the contact information of the cost segregation firm from that investor friend and promptly gets in touch with them. After paying $2,000 for the project, he can't wait to show the result to his CPA. The cost segregation resulted in over $80,000 of additional depreciation. This will surely save Edward a nice chunk of change in taxes, or so he thinks. To his disappointment, the CPA says that although there was accelerated depreciation, Edward will not be able to use the depreciation from his rental properties to offset his W-2 income. The reason? Edward makes too much money. Because Edward is making over $150,000 of income and is not eligible to claim real estate professional status, the accelerated depreciation will not result in a single dollar of tax savings for Edward this year.

Edward can't believe this. Why hadn't the cost segregation firm told him this before he paid them? Well, there is a perfectly good reason. The cost segregation firm is great at accelerating depreciation. However, they are not Edward's CPAs, and they are not preparing Edward's tax return. As such, they don't have insight as to how or whether the accelerated depreciation will benefit Edward. What Edward should have done was first talk with his CPA to find out if cost segregation would be a good strategy for him that year. If so, Edward could have had his CPA and the cost segregation firm work as a team to see if there were ways to best utilize this strategy.

The good news is that Edward did not lose out on that depreciation: It can still be used to offset taxes from future rental income. There are additional planning strategies to help Edward claim real estate professional status in future years so that he will receive these additional tax savings. Nonetheless, the sad truth is that Edward will not receive any current-year benefit from the cost segregation, and he is out of pocket the $2,000 that he paid the cost segregation firm.

As you can see, different investors have different tax profiles. A strategy that works wonders for one investor may be completely worthless to another. The best action to take is to plan ahead and get the appropriate advice from your tax advisor before implementing any tax strategies.

Are You Already Claiming It?

Cost segregation is another one of those frequently overlooked opportunities for real estate investors. There are lots of different ways to calculate depreciation, and it is somewhat rare that we see a tax return with depreciation done in a way that accelerates the depreciation deduction strategically. Why? Because not all CPAs are well versed in real estate. Further, the vast majority of tax return preparers may not have been taught cost segregation in school.

For most of the tax returns we review, we see investors who depreciate their rental property with two components: land and building. Depending on the investor's tax profile, this could hurt the investor when it comes to depreciation write-offs. Most rental properties have many more components than just simply land and building—there may be appliances, parking structures, landscaping, furniture, fixtures. These items can be depreciated much faster than land and building.

Accelerated depreciation is commonly discussed in the real estate world. Often, an investor may assume that their CPA is taking accelerated depreciation when it was not actually claimed on the tax return. If you feel you should have taken accelerated depreciation but are unsure whether that was actually done, one quick way to confirm is to take a look at the depreciation details in your last year's tax return. If you do not see anything listed other than the land and building for the property, it could make sense to meet with your CPA to determine if a cost segregation study might benefit you. By the same token, if you have made improvements to your property or if you purchased a recently rehabbed property, make sure to provide your tax advisor with the improvement breakouts so that they can help you accelerate your tax deduction when appropriate.

WHAT DOES IT ALL MEAN?

Depreciation is one of the best tax benefits of being a real estate investor. If used correctly, it can help reduce taxes from rental income as well as other types of income. One way to supercharge your depreciation deduction is to accelerate depreciation with a cost segregation study. The cost segregation study pushes future depreciation into the current year so that you can pay less tax now rather than waiting to pay less tax in future years.

There are a lot of myths and misconceptions with respect to cost segregation that should be noted. Before implementing a cost segregation study on your investment properties, make sure you meet with your tax advisor to determine whether it is a good strategy for your unique situation. If so, then a cost/benefit analysis should be done so that you can make an informed decision on whether this strategy will result in actual dollars saved.

CHAPTER 3

DEMYSTIFYING THE REAL ESTATE PROFESSIONAL TAX BENEFITS

"A penny saved is worth two pennies earned . . .
after taxes."

—RANDY THURMAN

On the outside, they seem to have the perfect life. Darin is a pediatric oncologist with two thriving medical offices. Jamie is a stay-at-home mom who spends a lot of her time shuffling their sons back and forth among different sports and after-school activities. Their four boys Ben, Kyle, Gavin, and Ethan excel in school and play various sports.

Between long days seeing patients in the office and emergency calls in the middle of the night, Darin realizes that the pressure from his career has taken a toll on his health. In the blink of an eye, his kids will soon be entering high school. Before long, they will be going away to college. Knowing how precious and fleeting time can be, Darin makes a New Year's resolution to work less, spend more time with his kids, and dedicate more time to his own health.

This, of course, is easier said than done. Even for a thriving physician, working less means making less money. With the high cost of college increasing every year, Darin needs to find a way to work less without losing too much of his bottom line. As Darin starts to comb through his finances, he's shocked to find that one of his biggest expense items each year isn't his mortgage payment or the kids' extracurricular costs. It isn't even his hobby of rebuilding classic cars. In fact, Darin's single biggest expense each year is income taxes.

While making just over $400,000 annually, Darin is losing close to $190,000 in taxes every year—federal income taxes, state income taxes, payroll taxes, property taxes, and sales tax. After seeing the whole picture more clearly, Darin thinks, *What if I can make money without working more hours and keep more of my hard-earned cash instead of losing it to taxes?*

Darin's next-door neighbor Fred is a retired firefighter and real estate investor. Fred always talks about how real estate provides passive income that makes his life more enjoyable in retirement. Fred once told Darin that not only did he avoid paying taxes on his rental income, but his CPA also helped him use rental tax benefits to reduce the taxes he paid on his pension income from the fire department.

As Darin thinks back to his casual conversations with Fred, he realizes that real estate is the solution he needs. He begins researching real estate, and it isn't long before he finds some rental properties a few miles outside of town that might be worth looking into. With a $30,000 down payment, Darin can purchase a 3-bedroom, 2-bathroom property for $150,000. The property will rent for $1,400 per month. After mortgage interest, property taxes, and some repairs and holding costs, the property will cash flow about $300 per month.

If Darin purchases five properties in a year, that can mean $1,500 of additional cash flow from the rentals each month. There is also news that the city is planning a revitalization project in the surrounding area, so if things go well, these properties can appreciate in value in the next few years, as well. The most enticing part of the real estate investing plan for Darin, though, is that he will be able to reduce his time in the medical practice, provided that the rental properties will replace some of that lost income.

His wife, Jamie, is very happy to hear that Darin wants to spend more time with family and focus on his health. She knows that Darin won't be able to drastically reduce his time in the medical practice immediately and that it will be a slow transition. Meanwhile, Jamie is happy to take the lead on the real estate business since the boys are getting older and more self-sufficient. In fact, Jamie considers this new adventure something that they can take on as a family and maybe even get the boys involved in the process.

After a few months of learning the ins and outs of real estate investing, Darin and Jamie decide to take the plunge and buy two rental properties just outside of the city. Not everything is seamless, of course. The houses need some light repairs, which Jamie finds contactors, plumbers, and electricians to fix. The for-rent ad they place online doesn't generate too much interest initially, so Jamie makes flyers and posts them on the bulletin boards of nearby restaurants and supermarkets. Just a few weeks later, they are able to place some good tenants in both rentals with long-term rental contracts. Now that the first two rentals are in full operation with cash flow coming in each month, Darin and Jamie decide to jump in and buy three more properties. By the end of the year, they are the proud owners of five rentals with cash flow of about $1,500 per month.

Since the rentals are operating well, Jamie is busy looking for more properties. Darin, on the other hand, is looking forward to tax time and excited to cash in on the tax savings of owning rental properties. For the first time in as long as he can remember, Darin is excited to meet with his tax person, Bob. He's excited to hear about all the great savings he'll receive now that he and Jamie are landlords.

To Darin's surprise, there won't be tax savings from his rentals. According to Bob, because their total income for the year is over $150,000, none of the rental expenses or losses will be available to offset Darin's medical income. This means that if Darin has a rental tax loss of $20,000 after maximizing his write-offs, the $20,000 rental loss won't help reduce the taxes from his medical income. Effectively, Darin will still continue to pay high taxes on all of his medical income, just like in the past.

Darin leaves Bob's office feeling defeated. He had hoped that the real estate portfolio he and Jamie were building would help them significantly reduce their taxes. According to Bob, the only reason neighbor Fred was able to see all the tax benefits of being a real estate investor was likely because Fred was retired with an income under $150,000.

Darin has been working with Bob for over a decade and knows plenty of other doctor colleagues who go to him as well. Darin is fairly certain that Bob knows what he's talking about—after all, Bob has been a licensed CPA for more than thirty years and is well-respected among the medical professionals in town.

Darin heads home to break the bad news to Jamie. That evening, they spend a few hours on the internet to see if they can find more information on exactly how rental real estate can help offset taxes for investors. Some sources affirm what Bob told them, while others indicate that it is still possible to benefit from real estate deductions even if you make income over that threshold.

Darin knows what he is good at and what he is not good at. He's good at being a medical doctor in pediatric oncology. He also knows that he is not good at accounting and tax law. Rather than sorting through all the various articles and blogs about real estate taxes, he decides to get the contact information for Fred's tax advisor, Mason, who apparently specializes in working with real estate investors. They want to meet with Mason just to get a second opinion. Maybe Mason will tell them the same exact things that Bob told them—after all, there's no reason for Bob to lie to them.

After initial pleasantries, Darin quickly tells Mason the purpose of the appointment. To their surprise, Mason actually disagrees with Bob's conclusion and instead teaches them a new strategy that allows them to use their new rentals to reduce Darin's medical income.

Using Rental Losses to Offset Ordinary Income

Mason first agrees that, in fact, the tax code can limit how rental losses are used when a taxpayer makes over $150,000 of adjusted gross income. If both spouses are working full-time and investing in real estate on the side, it is possible that any rental tax losses will not be used to offset non-rental income such as W-2, dividends, and capital gains.

In the tax world, these are known as passive activity loss rules. Basically, if you have passive losses from an activity such as rental real estate, those losses can only be used to offset other passive income. Generally speaking, passive losses, such as rental losses, cannot be used to offset taxes from ordinary income activities, such as W-2 income—not once a taxpayer's total adjusted gross income reaches $150,000. All hope is not lost, however. The way around this limitation, as explained by Mason, is with the real estate professional status.

Let's assume that Jamie is able to claim real estate professional status. This means that all rental expenses, depreciation, and net losses from the rentals can be used to offset rental income. In addition to that, any excess losses from the properties can also be used to offset Darin's medical income. So if Darin makes medical income of $400,000, and they have rental tax losses after depreciation of $50,000, Darin and Jamie will pay taxes only on $350,000 of total income. Assuming a combined federal and state income tax rate of 45 percent, this can mean actual taxes saved of up to $22,500 per year.

Darin and Jamie are excited about this new potential strategy. Saving $22,500 in taxes means a lot less time that Darin has to work in the medical practice. But they have a lot of questions. First, how can they become real estate professionals? After all, Darin is a physician and Jamie was an engineer before deciding to become a stay-at-home mom. Neither of them have ever been a Realtor or sold properties.

Who Can Be a Real Estate Professional?

What exactly is a real estate professional, and how exactly does someone qualify for that designation? The truth is, neither Darin nor Jamie are really interested in getting a Realtor's license and giving up their weekends to hold open houses.

Contrary to popular belief, you do not have to be in the business of selling real estate, be an agent, work under a broker, or show houses for sale. In fact, you don't even have to be licensed as a Realtor. *Real estate professional status* is a term that exists only in the tax world as defined by the IRS. It has nothing to do with the degree you went to school for, nor which licenses you may hold. Alternatively, just because you are licensed in real estate does not automatically mean you are eligible to be a real estate professional in the eyes of the IRS. To receive the tax benefits of being a real estate professional, you simply must meet the hour and participation requirements of the IRS.

Requirement #1

The person claiming real estate professional status must spend at least 750 hours in qualified real estate professional activities as defined by the IRS. This time is calculated on an annual basis from January 1 to December 31, so the time is not required based on a weekly or monthly basis. For example, it would be perfectly fine for Jamie to spend no real estate time in January through March, as long as she spends at least 750 hours for the rest of the year from April through December.

Requirement #2

That person must also spend more time in real estate than in their other jobs combined. Since Jamie was a stay-at-home mom and was not working to earn income from any other sources, she only needed to show being actively involved in real estate for 750 hours for the year to claim real estate professional status.

But what if Jamie decides to start a side business, such as working on freelance projects from home? She can still claim real estate professional status if she meets all the requirements. As an example, if Jamie spends 1,000 hours on her freelance business and spends 1,001 hours in real estate, then she can claim real estate professional status to receive the tax benefits. In that situation, she meets both requirements by spending at least 750 hours in real estate *and* spending more time in real estate than her side business.

Requirement #3

The time requirements above must be met by one taxpayer and cannot be a combined time of two individuals. In other words, Darin and Jamie cannot combine their real estate time to meet the 750-hour requirement. In order for Jamie to meet real estate professional status, she needs to meet both time requirements above on her own. Any time that Darin spends on real estate does not help Jamie achieve her 750-hour requirement.

Another important item to note is that real estate professional activities do not need to be specifically related to rental properties. For example, what if Jamie decides to get licensed as a Realtor to help others buy and sell properties? Or what if she decides to start her own side business managing properties for other investors in her local area? Maybe she decides that she loves the rehab process and starts flipping properties on her own. Does that qualify as real estate professional time? In all three of these scenarios, Jamie's time as an agent, property manager, or flipper can all count toward her time as a real estate professional, even though the work she's performing is not directly related to the five rentals she and Darin own.

Another great thing about real estate professional benefits is that, as soon as one of the couple meets the qualifications to claim real estate professional status, both receive the benefits. As a result, Jamie's ability to claim real estate professional status means that their rental losses can be used to offset Darin's medical income—even though Darin himself is not claiming to be a real estate professional.

Material Participation

Darin and Jamie like what they have heard so far. Since Darin is spending the majority of his time practicing medicine, Jamie is already the lead on most real estate–related activities anyhow. Before receiving the tax benefits of investing in rental real estate, Jamie and Darin need to meet another test.

In addition to meeting the qualifications for real estate professional status, an investor also needs to be able to show that they "materially participate" in the rental properties that they own. Material participation is defined as the taxpayer being involved in the operations of their real estate in a regular, continuous, and substantial way. The IRS has seven tests that may be used to determine whether the taxpayer meets the requirement, and they can be found in Appendix B. You only need to meet one of the seven tests in order to qualify for material participation. One of the most commonly used is the 500-hour test—the taxpayer needs to spend at least 500 hours during the year materially participating in their rental properties.

Although material participation is limited to time spent on properties owned by the investor, time incurred by both spouses can be combined to meet this 500-hour requirement. If Jamie spends 400 hours on the rentals and Darin spends 100 hours on their rentals, they would meet the 500-hour test for material participation.

Documentation

How exactly do you prove your time spent on real estate to the IRS? As with many things in the tax world, it all comes down to documentation. The IRS requires that the taxpayer keep a log of the real estate activities that were done during the year. There is no specific method to keep track of the activities—the time log can be kept using an online calendar, a time-tracking app, an Excel workbook, or it can be handwritten in a notebook.

The IRS does require that the time log be kept using a consistent method for the entire year. They don't like time logs that are partially kept in a notebook, partially in Excel, and partially on a calendar. The time log should also be kept and maintained throughout the year because the IRS gives more weight to time logs that are completed while you are incurring the time versus time logs that people try to create after the fact.

Some of the items that should be in a real estate professional's time log include the date, a description of the activity performed (as specific and detailed as possible), the duration of the activity, and the related property address.

For example:

03/01/19 • Met with property manager to view repairs proposal • 3321 Main St rental • 2 hours

From an audit protection perspective, it's recommended that your real estate professional time log includes activities that can be verified and substantiated. In the event of an audit, the IRS may ask to review your time log and it may take sample selections for testing. If your time log is made up of, say, 200 logged entries, they may take a random sampling of ten entries and request that you prove time spent on those activities. Be sure to keep copies of emails, phone calls, text messages, receipts, car mileage, and other documentation that can help prove your case in the event of an IRS audit.

Of course, not everything can be proven with paperwork. What about the time that you happened to drop in on an open house and ended up chatting with a Realtor who ultimately sold you another rental property? There may be no emails or prior correspondence to prove that you were there, just a flyer or Realtor's business card that you grabbed from the table. Just make sure to apply the "reasonableness test" when recording your time. If you were sitting across the table from an IRS auditor and making your case, would it be reasonable if you told them that you stopped by an open house unexpectedly and chatted with the Realtor for an hour or so to find out more about that property for sale? Probably. Would it be reasonable that you spent five hours chatting with this Realtor at the open house? Probably not.

There are right and wrong ways to keep track of your time for real estate professional status. First, the IRS does not like ballpark estimates of time. The time spent must also be credible. For example, an IRS auditor disallowed a taxpayer's claim that he spent 24 hours to replace 4 window blinds, 56 hours to replace a toilet, and 280 hours to close the books of his rental properties. Believe it or not, the IRS has caught taxpayers who logged more than 24 hours of real estate activities in a single day.

If you are trying to claim real estate professional status while working a full-time job, be very careful and detailed about how you track your time. It is often difficult for an investor with a full-time job outside of real estate to be able to show more time was spent in real estate. For example, if you are an investor who worked full-time at your W-2 job with 2,100 hours for the year, you must spend at least 2,101 hours in real estate in order to claim real estate professional status. But suppose you are very efficient at your job? What if you get paid to work eight hours a day but you can do your job in three hours, and the rest of your workday you sit at your desk and search for real estate deals online? Unfortunately, the IRS still deems that to be an eight-hour workday, so efficiency does not reduce the work hours for real estate professional purposes.

What is the right way to document time? Here's an example: A commercial boat pilot was able to successfully prove that he spent more time fixing up his rental properties than he spent as a boat pilot. He kept credible and detailed logs on the work that he performed. The pilot was able to show the before-and-after pictures of the work he had done on the rental and had witnesses testify to his extraordinary work ethic. The IRS found his time log to be credible and reasonable and allowed his claim as a real estate professional, although he also earned income outside of real estate.

Benefits Comparison

Remember Darin and Jamie? Over this past year, with the five new rentals they purchased, Jamie has definitely spent at least 750 hours in real estate activities, including meeting the 500-hour material participation test, and she can easily document the time she spent. Mason is also recommending that they do cost segregation to accelerate the depreciation on all of their new rentals. Accelerated depreciation will allow them to push up the depreciation expense into the current year by breaking out the components of each of the five rental buildings.

With accelerated depreciation, their projected net tax loss from their rentals is now estimated to be $67,000. Here is a comparison of Darin and Jamie's tax bill with and without real estate professional status:

	Taxes Without Real Estate Professional Status	Taxes With Real Estate Professional Status
Total Medical Income	$400,000	$400,000
Rental Income After Expenses	$18,000	$18,000
Accelerated Depreciation	($85,000)	($85,000)
Net Rental Loss	($67,000)	($67,000)
Total Taxable Income	$400,000	$333,000
Total Federal and State Tax Rates	45%	45%
Total Taxes	$180,000	$149,850
Total Annual Tax Savings		**$30,150**

*This is typically how accountants write charts. All numbers inside parenthesis are a loss, or negative, throughout the book.

By claiming real estate professional status for Jamie, the $67,000 of rental losses can be used to offset Darin's medical income. This helps them save $30,150 of cash in just the first year!

Most Common Tax Mistakes

For Darin and Jamie, the difference between claiming real estate professional status and not claiming real estate professional status is a significant amount, $30,150. They really want to know why Bob hadn't told them about this strategy. After all, Bob is a well-respected tax advisor in the medical profession.

According to Mason, missing the real estate professional designation is one of the most common tax mistakes that he sees as a real estate CPA. Bob was not deliberately lying to Darin and Jamie—he just didn't take the next step to determine whether Jamie could have claimed real estate professional status. Even though real estate provides some great tax benefits, you still need a CPA who has enough knowledge and experience to be able to uncover some of these hidden benefits.

This is probably the most common and costly tax mistake made by real estate investors because it's not as simple as listing "real estate professional" as your occupation on the tax return. There is no box to check or form to fill out. In fact, claiming the real estate professional status is almost trickier than qualifying for it.

One of the hidden traps relates to the material participation requirement. As we discussed, as part of qualifying to be a real estate professional, a taxpayer needs to materially participate in their own rentals. But this requirement actually applies to *each* rental property the taxpayer owns. Remember, there are seven tests a taxpayer can use to pass the material participation test shown in Appendix B, but all these tests are supposed to be applied separately to *each* rental property.

As an example, let's assume a taxpayer wants to use the 500-hour material participation test. Therefore, in Darin and Jamie's example, since they own five rentals, this means that they need to spend 2,500 hours on their rental properties before they can receive the tax benefits of being a real estate professional. One way to avoid this requirement is to make and include an election (see Appendix C) with your tax return that includes specific language to aggregate your rental properties as one single activity. By making that election, this means that you only need to show 500 hours *total* for all your rentals combined for the year to pass the material participation test. Without this election, the IRS would require the 500-hour test to be met by each rental property separately.

To many investors, and even CPAs, this requirement makes no sense. Why does the IRS require a piece of paper to be attached to the tax return in order have all rentals treated as one property for the time requirement? This has been perhaps one of the most misunderstood and most controversial aspects of the real estate professional rules between taxpayers and the IRS. As ludicrous as it may seem, it is extremely important to make sure the election is included in the tax return filed with the IRS. There have been many cases where the investor would have otherwise qualified for the hours' requirement, but the IRS disallowed the tax deduction simply because the election was not attached to the return.

If you feel that you should have been claiming real estate professional status, you should double-check with your tax advisor. In addition, you should look at your previous years' tax returns to see if you can spot an election to aggregate your rental properties attached to your tax return.

The IRS did release legislation that says for certain taxpayers, it may be possible to file amended tax returns for the real estate professional status if it was done incorrectly. To claim real estate professional status on your tax return the right way, make sure to keep these items in mind:

- Have a log book to accurately track your time during the year. Although this is not attached to your tax return, it should be retained for your records in the event of an IRS audit.
- Make sure you list your occupation on the tax return as a real estate professional.
- If you own more than one rental property, make sure you include an election to aggregate your rentals into a single activity.
- Ensure that the return is being calculated to allow any rental losses to offset your other non-rental income.

In Darin and Jamie's case, investing in rental real estate helped them increase their cash flow by $1,500 per month—and without the need for Darin to work harder in his medical practice. The additional $30,150 in tax savings in just the first year means even more money in their pockets—which can be a down payment on another rental property that can generate even more cash flow and even more tax savings every year. Darin and Jamie learned that claiming the real estate professional status correctly could be the biggest tax saving strategy for them each and every year.

WHAT DOES IT ALL MEAN?

Many investors making over $150,000 per year may not be able to use their rental losses each year to offset taxes generated from other income activities. However, the limitation may be avoided if the taxpayer can qualify as a real estate professional. Don't let the name mislead you— real estate professional does not mean you have to be licensed as a professional Realtor or broker. You just need to meet the time and activities requirements as dictated in the tax law.

Once a person qualifies as a real estate professional, rental losses can be used to reduce taxes from all sorts of income, including W-2, interest, dividends, capital gains, social security income, and retirement distributions.

The key to successfully claiming real estate professional status is to have accurate and detailed logs on the time that you spend in real estate activities. Not claiming real estate professional status correctly and not including the right elections with your tax return are two of the most costly tax mistakes made by real estate investors. Make sure to file your taxes the right way!

CHAPTER 4

HOW TO SAVE ON TAXES EVEN WHEN YOU'RE NOT A REAL ESTATE PROFESSIONAL

"Life keeps throwing me stones. And I keep finding the diamonds . . . "

—ANA CLAUDIA ANTUNES

The ability to claim as a real estate professional clearly has its tax benefits. But what if your income is over $150,000 and you do not meet the requirements to claim real estate professional status? What if you have a full-time job and do not spend more time in real estate than your job? What if you only have one out-of-state turnkey rental that is taken care of by a property management company and you spend virtually no time on this passive rental property? Does it mean there are no tax benefits to investing in real estate for you? Of course not.

Sam retired from being a high school principal at age 55. Although he doesn't want to go back to teaching full-time, he misses being an educator. A local tutoring company contacts him and offers him a position to work a few hours a week to help high school kids prepare for college entrance exams. In addition to working part-time as a tutor, Sam also starts to get into real estate investing. For his first rental property, Sam wants to start out small and buys a turnkey property in his home state. Sam wants to buy a fully rehabbed property with a tenant already in place so that he can test the waters with real estate investing. He also wants to learn the ins and outs of being an investor without doing everything on his own.

During his first year as a real estate investor, the rental property generates a good amount of cash flow. After writing off all the legitimate business expenses related to his rental property and claiming depreciation, Sam's rental results in a small tax loss of close to $14,000.

Rental Income	$18,400
Expenses	
Taxes	($1,800)
Interest	($7,200)
Property Management Expense	($1,800)
Repairs Expense	($500)
Travel/Meals/Home Office	($3,100)
Net Rental Income	**$4,000**
Depreciation	($18,000)
Net Tax Loss	**($14,000)**

Between his retirement pension income and the income from his part-time tutoring job, his total income is just over $150,000. After tallying up his time log, it turns out that Sam only spent about 600 hours on real estate during the year. Since Sam doesn't meet the 750-hour requirement, he is not able to claim real estate professional status, and as a result, he isn't able to use the $14,000 rental losses to offset the taxes from his pension and W-2 income. Before you get too sad for Sam, here are some important things to know with respect to his situation.

Offsetting Taxes from Rental Income

First, even though Sam isn't able to use rental losses to offset his pension and W-2 income, he is able to use all of his rental expenses to offset rental income. In fact, Sam will pay zero taxes on his rental income of $18,400 after claiming all his rental-related expenses and depreciation.

Owning Multiple Rentals

What if Sam had owned two properties in that first year? For example, if Property 1 had a tax loss but Property 2 had taxable income? They could be used to offset each other. One way for Sam to maximize his tax benefit from real estate investing might be to purchase more rentals so that he can have more tax-free or tax-efficient rental income.

	Property 1	Property 2
Rental Income	**$18,400**	**$23,000**
Expenses		
Taxes	($1,800)	($2,300)
Interest	($7,200)	—
Property Management Expense	($1,800)	($1,800)
Repairs Expense	($500)	($600)
Travel/Meals/Home Office	($3,100)	($200)
Net Rental Income	**$4,000**	**$18,100**
Depreciation	($18,000)	($9,000)
Net Tax Income/(Loss)	**($14,000)**	**$9,100**
Total Tax Loss	**($14,000) + $9,100 =**	**($4,900)**

Syndication Investments

In fact, if Sam is interested in being a passive investor in someone else's deal, then he will be able to use his rental property loss to offset the gain on that investment, as well. For example, what if Sam's friend is a real estate guru who put together an LLC that invests in a great cash-flowing apartment syndication? If Sam invests in his friend's LLC and that LLC generates rental income for Sam, Sam can use the loss from his turnkey rental to offset or even eliminate the taxes on his income from the apartment syndication.

Short-Term Rentals

What if Sam decides to get into the business of short-term rental investing? Let's say that Sam buys another 3-bedroom, 2-bathroom property close to the shore and decides he can make four times more money than renting it out to a long-term tenant? The rental loss from his turnkey property can also be used to offset taxable income from his short-term rental properties.

As you can see, not claiming real estate professional status doesn't prohibit Sam from using rental losses from his turnkey property to offset other sources of rental income. As such, one of the best ways to utilize rental losses is to simply work hard to generate more rental income. After all, wasn't that your main goal when you decided to invest in real estate?

Different Years, Different Results

After investing in the turnkey property, Sam starts to attend local real estate club meetings and begins networking with other local real estate investors. Sam learns that by buying properties that need a little TLC, he will generate better returns than by purchasing more properties from a turnkey provider.

In his second year of investing, Sam purchases a duplex that needs a little bit of rehab. Of course, things don't always turn out as planned—Sam's light rehab of new paint and carpet for the duplex ends up being more work than expected. In addition to painting the inside of the property, Sam decides to redo the flooring in both units and to repaint the outside of the duplex to give it a face-lift. Instead of paying to get the work done, Sam decides to save money by doing all the work himself.

All the hours of sweat equity that Sam puts into the duplex really turn out well. In fact, he is able to get both units rented out quickly at a price slightly higher than what the prior property owner had charged.

As with the previous year, Sam tallies up his hours in real estate activities and determines that, between his turnkey property and the new duplex, he has spent close to 1,000 hours in real estate activities during the year. Comparatively, Sam worked about 800 hours that year as a part-time tutor for the college prep students. Because Sam spent over

750 hours in real estate and he spent more time in real estate than his job as a tutor, he is finally able to qualify as a real estate professional in his second year as a real estate investor. As a real estate professional, Sam is able to use his rental losses from the turnkey rental and the duplex to offset taxes from his pension income.

Real estate professional is a year-by-year designation. Sam was not a real estate professional in Year One, but that doesn't mean he can't be in Year Two. Conversely, just because Sam meets the requirements to claim real estate professional in Year Two, that doesn't mean he will automatically qualify in Year Three. He still needs to meet the hours and activities requirements for Year Three in order to receive the tax benefits. Eligibility is determined strictly on the amount of time and the type of activities that the investor is involved in, with respect to real estate transactions for any given year.

Is Real Estate Professional Status Helpful for All Investors?

Should it be every investor's goal to qualify as a real estate professional? Not necessarily. There are times when it may provide little to no benefits for certain investors.

Taxable Income Versus Tax Loss

Back to Sam's example. Let's fast-forward ten years down the road to when Sam might have paid off the loans on his rentals and will no longer have mortgage interest. Maybe he has accelerated all the depreciation deductions and has little left to claim on his tax returns. What if Sam doesn't have an overall rental loss during the year? In years where Sam has a taxable rental income instead of a tax loss, real estate professional becomes a moot point. The main benefit of being a real estate professional is the ability to use rental losses to offset other types of non-rental income. Without tax rental losses, there is no tax need for Sam to claim real estate professional status.

Other Types of Real Estate Income

As you know, not all real estate investors own rental properties. Real estate investors generate income from all types of different sources, and they each have very different tax treatments. If you're an investor who generates only fix-and-flip profit, there is no benefit to claiming real estate professional status. Why? Because you have no rental income. Flip profit is considered ordinary income in the tax world and not rental income. As mentioned earlier, being a real estate professional is helpful for those who have *rental* losses. Since flip profit is not a rental loss, there is no benefit for a flipper to claim real estate professional status.

What if you generate only wholesale income? Just like flip income, wholesale income is not a rental, so it is not impacted by real estate professional status. Trust deed lenders also are not impacted by real estate professional status because trust deed investors typically generate interest income. Again, it is not a rental loss; there is no impact from the real estate professional standpoint.

On the other hand, what if you are a flipper, wholesaler, or trust deed investor who also happens to invest in rental real estate? In that case, it might benefit you to claim real estate professional status if you have rental losses, as they could be used to offset your ordinary income.

Income and Losses Below Threshold

As discussed previously, those with income over the $150,000 threshold are limited in their ability to use rental losses to offset other non-rental income unless real estate professional status is claimed. But what about investors who have income under $150,000? Well, there is some good news for investors below that threshold: A special rule allows certain taxpayers to use up to $25,000 of rental losses to offset non-rental income each year, even if they do not qualify as a real estate professional.

Active Participation

In order to benefit from this rule, the investor must be able to show that they are "actively" involved in real estate. Active participation is a lot less stringent than the requirements of real estate professional. Unlike real estate professional status requirements, the investor is not required to have regular, continuous, and substantial involvement in the real estate to claim active participation. They just need to be making management decisions or arranging for others to provide services for the properties. Activities that qualify under the active participation rule can include simple tasks such as approving new tenants, setting rental terms and policies, or simply approving repairs, expenses, or improvement costs.

For example, let's assume Sam's turnkey is an out-of-state rental instead of a local one. Sam collects rent checks by mail and does not travel to see the rental property at all for the entire year. When repairs are needed, Sam hires people to do the repair work. When tenants move out, Sam decides who the new tenant will be and sets the policy and rental prices. Because Sam makes all the management decisions and has others perform the services, Sam is deemed to be actively involved in the real estate even though he does not physically visit the property.

Income Phaseout

For investors who have a modified adjusted gross income under $100,000, up to $25,000 of rental losses can be used to offset other non-rental income. This means that if you had $90,000 of W-2 income and $25,000 of rental losses, you may offset these amounts and only pay taxes on $65,000 of income.

Total modified adjusted gross income: $90,000

Rental losses allowed: −$25,000

Total taxable income: $65,000

If your income exceeds $100,000, a 50 percent phaseout will be calculated. Between $100,000 and $150,000, investors may receive partial benefit from the ability to use rental losses to offset other non-rental income. Once modified adjusted gross income exceeds $150,000, the entire $25,000 of rental losses are phased out and can no longer be used to offset non-rental income.

Total modified adjusted gross income: $150,000

Rental losses allowed: $25,000 − ([$150,000 − $100,000] × 50%) = **$0**

Total taxable income: $150,000

Additional Planning Strategies

Because adjusted gross income determines how rental losses can be used to offset taxes, there are many planning opportunities to utilize. At the heart of it all, the goal is to reduce total adjusted gross income below the $150,000 mark. The closer it can be reduced to $100,000, the better the potential tax benefits.

Debbie works as a compliance manager at an investment firm; she makes a little over $100,000 of income. She purchased a small rental property about three years ago in Scottsdale, Arizona. Debbie's rental was fairly hassle-free, and she was fortunate to have the same great tenants for the past three years. In addition to the monthly cash flow from the tenant that was deposited into Debbie's bank account, Debbie also enjoyed the tax benefits of her rental property. For the past three years, Debbie has been able to use depreciation and her other rental expenses to reduce taxes from her W-2 income at work.

But as they say, all good things must come to an end. In late April, Debbie's tenants gave her notice that they would be moving. Due to a new job opportunity, they were relocating out of state. Although Debbie is sad to see her long-term tenants go, she is looking forward to spending some time in Arizona this summer. Debbie's mom retired a year previously and moved to live in Scottsdale to take advantage of the warm weather. Debbie plans to take a few weeks off from her job to work on the rental property. It needs some new carpet, painting, and fixtures and hardware before new tenants can move in. In addition to working on the property, she will also get to spend some good quality time with her mom.

From travel costs, supplies, and other repair costs, Debbie incurs a significant number of expenses relating to her rental property. She also gets a raise at work, and her W-2 income is now $152,000. Because Debbie's income is now over the $150,000 threshold, she will not be able to use rental losses to offset taxes from her W-2 job. As you may have guessed, Debbie doesn't qualify as a real estate professional because she doesn't spend more time on her rental than her full-time job. Fortunately, her tax advisor tells her that she could change her situation.

By making contributions to her work retirement account, Debbie will be able to reduce her total income to be able to receive some tax benefits from her rental properties. After depreciation and rental expenses, Debbie is projected to have a tax loss of $8,000 for her rental property for the tax year. If she makes retirement contributions of $19,000 to her work 401(k) plan, she will reduce her income down to the threshold where all her rental losses can be used to reduce taxes from her W-2 income.

	Without 401(k)	With 401(k)
W-2 Income	$152,000	$152,000
401(k) Contributions	—	($19,000)
Total Income	$152,000	$133,000
Rental Losses Allowed	— *	($8,500) **
Total Taxable Income	**$152,000**	**$124,500**

*$25,000 – ([$152,000 – $100,000] × 50%) = $0
**$25,000 – ([$133,000 – $100,000] × 50%) = $8,500

Debbie's 401(k) contributions help reduce her total taxable income. In addition, it allows her to use an additional $8,500 of rental losses to offset her total taxable income when it would otherwise be disallowed. The $8,500 rental loss helps her save an additional $2,890 in federal and state income taxes based on her 34 percent tax rate.

It is important to take note that using a 401(k) is not the only way to reduce total taxable income. When planning to lower total income, it's important to look at all other types of strategies designed to reduce your overall taxes. Analyzing your entire financial profile and taking a holistic planning approach with your tax advisor can often uncover these little hidden tax gems.

Common Myths About Real Estate Professional Status

Professional Designations
Investors are often confused by what needs to be done to qualify as a real estate professional. Because this is such a common misconception, it is worth mentioning again: You are not required to be licensed in real estate in order to claim real estate professional status. You simply must meet the time and activities requirements as described by the IRS.

Legal Entities
Another very common myth we hear from investors is the need to have legal entities in order to claim real estate professional status. That is also incorrect. Real estate professional status is a designation claimed by the individual, not an entity. In fact, an entity cannot claim to be a real es-

tate professional. Why? Because how can a legal entity "spend time" on real estate? A person can spend time in real estate on behalf of the entity and that could count toward time for that "person" to claim real estate professional status.

Let's go over an example: Ian owns a rental property on Main Street in his personal name that he purchased many years ago. When Ian spends time on the Main Street property, that can count toward real estate professional time. Ian also owns 100 percent of an LLC that holds a fourplex rental. Ian's time spent on the fourplex in the LLC also can count toward real estate professional status and time. When qualifying for the time and activities test, Ian's time on his rental properties is calculated the same exact way, regardless of whether it was related to his personally held rentals or the rentals held in his LLC.

Writing Off Expenses

Another common myth we hear from investors is the assumption that certain expenses can only be claimed when the investor is considered a real estate professional. However, legitimate expenses relating to your real estate investment are deductible regardless of your income level and ability to claim real estate professional. This means that if you attend a local real estate club meeting, that is still a legitimate expense to be claimed on your tax return. Same for real estate–related car expenses, travel costs, meals, education costs, home office, and much more.

We have also often heard from investors who were told by their tax advisors that they cannot claim depreciation because they are not real estate professionals. This is also incorrect. Depreciation is just like any other rental expense and can be claimed each and every year that the property is operating as a rental. In fact, the IRS requires landlords to take depreciation on the rental property, so make sure you are claiming that every year on your taxes.

As long as the expense is ordinary and necessary as it relates to your real estate investment activities, it should be tracked and claimed on your tax return. The only difference is that, in years where your income exceeds the threshold and you are not a real estate professional, those losses simply do not offset other income, such as your W-2 income.

What Happens to the Unallowed Losses?

What happens to all those expenses and losses if you can't use them to offset your other sources of income? Well, at least you do not lose out on the deductions. Instead, they are carried forward into future years and can be used to offset future rental income, as well as capital gains from future sales of rental properties. In addition, as discussed previously, the carryforward rental losses from one property can be used to offset future rental income of another property. The same goes for capital gains.

Let's say that I own Rental Property A and that it had $10,000 of rental losses I claimed on my return. And let's assume I am not able to use those losses to offset my W-2 income this year. Next year, if I sell Rental Property B for a capital gain of $50,000, I could use the $10,000 rental loss from Rental Property A to offset Rental Property B's capital gain. At the end of the day, I would only pay taxes on $40,000.

What if I only own Rental Property A and I accumulated rental losses of $30,000 over the years that I couldn't use because of an inability to claim real estate professional status? When I sell Rental Property A, I would be able to use the entire $30,000 accumulated rental loss to offset my non-rental income (such as W-2, interest, capital gains). For example, if I make $200,000 at my job and I sell my rental in a year where my accumulated rental losses carried forward were $30,000, I would pay taxes on only $170,000 that year. This is true even though my income is above the $150,000 threshold and I am working full-time and not claiming real estate professional status. Assuming a tax rate of 42 percent, this could save me over $12,000 in taxes.

This is an important item to note because, even though I may not have benefited from my rental expenses over the years, I would ultimately get to benefit from all my write-offs that had been accumulating over the years when I sold the property. We often hear from clients who complain that although they are diligent in tracking all the rental-related expenses, they are not seeing any tax savings when they file their tax returns. This is because they continue to pay high taxes on their W-2 income. Wouldn't it be easier if they just stopped tracking all the rental expenses each year? The answer is absolutely not. As an investor, we always want to capture and maximize our rental expenses because those expenses will need to be claimed on the tax returns each year in order to be used to offset taxes from our future income. If the expenses are not captured and claimed on the tax returns each year, that tax benefit is lost forever!

WHAT DOES IT ALL MEAN?

Tax benefits from rental investing are eligible to all investors. Rentals are often one of the most tax-efficient sources of income, even for those with higher income who are just investing on the side. Because rental losses from one property or entity can be used to offset rental income from another property or another entity, it is important to make sure that we focus on generating as much cash flow as possible to be able to utilize our rental deductions. Real estate professional is a year-by-year designation, so not qualifying in Year One does not preclude you from qualifying in future years. Generally speaking, the more rentals you own, the easier it may become for you to qualify for real estate professional status.

For those taxpayers with higher incomes above the IRS threshold, all hope is not lost. With proper tax planning, there are many other tax-saving tools that can be utilized together in order to achieve the lowest tax results possible. Additional strategies discussed in other chapters within this book, as well as many of the strategies discussed in our first book, *Tax Strategies for the Savvy Real Estate Investor*, may be used together to potentially help reduce your overall income so that you receive current tax benefits from your rentals, even if you may not qualify as a real estate professional. To make sure that you don't overpay the IRS, you must track all legitimate expenses related to your real estate business each and every year.

CHAPTER 5

SQUEEZING THE MOST TAX SAVINGS FROM YOUR SHORT-TERM RENTALS

"The avoidance of taxes is the only intellectual pursuit that still carries any reward."

—JOHN MAYNARD KEYNES

Short-term rentals have made a huge impact on the real estate investment community. Attend any real estate investment club or meeting and you are bound to meet a handful of investors who are in the short-term rentals space. Whether it is renting out their entire home while they are away, renting out part of their home, or simply renting out entire properties or buildings for a short term, the one recurring theme is this: Short-term rentals can produce more cash flow than traditional long-term rentals.

Short-term rentals do not necessarily mean you have to rent out your property on Airbnb or Vrbo. For example, there are investors who specialize in looking for properties close to airports. These types of properties may be ideal as short-term rentals for flight attendants who have overnight layovers. Rather than simply renting out the entire house to flight attendants, an investor might be able to make even more cash flow by renting out each room separately or even each bed. Other times, investors can increase cash flow by renting out properties that are close to hospitals. Whether it is to accommodate traveling patients and their families or renting to medical students on rotations, these short-term rentals can be a powerful tool to generate additional cash flow.

As CPAs, we often see investor clients double or even triple their rental income by turning a traditional rental into a short-term rental. Some investors wonder: How is that possible? Well, let's assume you have a property that generates income of $1,500 per month as a traditional long-term rental. If you turned it into a short-term rental on Airbnb and were able to charge an average of $150 per night, you could get $3,000 of rental income if you rented out the property for just twenty nights out of the month. Over the course of a year, that property could generate rental income of up to $36,000.

If you are an investor with a couple of short-term rentals, you can see that this great cash flow could result in some potential tax issues. The higher the income, the more planning you need to do to reduce or eliminate taxes on that income.

Brandon is itching to get into real estate. However, after just graduating from law school, he doesn't have enough money for a down payment to buy a property. For the past several months, Brandon has worked hard to save money for his first investment. He lived in a one-bedroom downtown apartment. His apartment was so close to the downtown football stadium that he and his friends would sometimes just walk to the games and save money on parking. His friends would often crash at his house after the games if they drank too much to drive home for the night. Being the nice host that he is, Brandon purchased a used futon for his living room so that it would be more comfortable for his friends when they did stay over.

As a lifetime football fan, Brandon was excited to find out that this year's Super Bowl game would take place at the stadium by his house. He knew he would not be able to attend the game because of the high cost of the tickets, but he was happy that he could have some friends over to watch the game and perhaps participate in the pregame festivities that would be sure to happen downtown.

That was the original plan, at least, until Brandon found out about a way he could make some money. One afternoon, Brandon was talking with a neighbor when he learned that the neighbor was renting out their unit through Airbnb for the big game. According to the neighbor, similar apartments in the area were renting for over $1,100 per night the week leading up to the game. As the dates got closer to the actual game, the prices increased accordingly to $1,800. Brandon could not believe that his little one-bedroom apartment could rent out for such a high price. When he went home, he immediately hopped online to look for himself.

According to Airbnb, Brandon could expect to make an average of $1,200 per night if he were to rent out his apartment for the Super Bowl game. The price was even higher than what his neighbor had told him because Brandon's living room futon allowed accommodation for an additional guest. If he were able to rent out his property for two weeks, Brandon might be able to make $16,800 in rental income. That was money he could use as a down payment on his first rental property.

The same afternoon, Brandon listed his apartment online as a short-term rental, and before the evening was over, he had rented out his apartment for two weeks through the Super Bowl.

Brandon decided to call his friend Chad, a CPA and a real estate investor, for three reasons. First, he needed to tell Chad that the Super Bowl party at his apartment would be canceled. Second, Brandon would need a place to stay for the two weeks that he rented his place, and third, Brandon wanted to ask Chad if there were any ways he could reduce taxes on the $16,800 of rental income. After all, money paid to the IRS meant less money for Brandon to invest into his first deal. Just with his legal income alone, Brandon was already paying taxes at close to 34 percent. Brandon was now afraid that this additional $16,800 of rental income might push him into the next tax bracket.

Tax-Free Rental Income

To Brandon's surprise, Chad had some great news. According to Chad, there would be no taxes assessed on the $16,800 of rental income because the apartment was Brandon's primary home and he was renting it out for fourteen days. Apparently the IRS has a loophole in which taxpayers who rent out their primary or vacation home can receive tax-free treatment as long as the property is rented out for fourteen days or less.

The other good news was that there are no restrictions on the dollar amount of rental income that could be tax-free. In other words, if Brandon were to rent out his apartment for $10,000 per night for fourteen nights, he would receive the entire $140,000 of rental income completely tax-free. Chad did issue a word of caution to Brandon, though: This tax-free treatment was only available if Brandon rented out his home for fourteen days or less. If he were to rent out his home for more than fourteen days, then the rental income would become completely taxable, just like any other rental real estate.

There was another small downside to all of this. Because this rental income would be tax-free, Brandon would not be able to write off any rental-related expenses on this property. So, if Brandon went out and bought new linens and supplies for his guests, he would not be able to write those off. Since Brandon was expecting to have very few expenses anyway, this would not adversely impact him too much. However, although overhead expenses were not deductible, Brandon's usual primary home deductions were still valid. As such, Brandon could still write off 100 percent of the mortgage interest and property taxes on his Schedule A, just as he would if he didn't have the rental income.

Brandon was on cloud nine when he found out that he would be able to keep all his rental income and pay none of it to the IRS. Chad did remind him that although the $16,800 is tax-free money to Brandon, it is still very likely that Airbnb would report this amount to the IRS. As such, Brandon might want to consider reporting the amount on his tax return so that it would match the IRS records and minimize any potential IRS inquiries. To avoid taxes being assessed on the tax return, Brandon could simply record a corresponding offset to reduce the income down to zero.

From that day on, Brandon fell in love with short-term rental investing. He saw how easy it could be done and how little time it took for him to be personally involved in the transactions. Besides getting the property ready for the guests, there wasn't really much for Brandon to do until the guests left and he had to go back in and clean up the place. With the $16,800 he had made, Brandon immediately purchased his very first rental property. Of course, his plan was to also operate it as a short-term rental. He remembered Chad's warning about the fourteen-day rule. Since he already rented out his home for fourteen days during the Super Bowl, would renting out the new property this year cause the $16,800 to now become taxable?

Fortunately, the answer was no. Renting out an investment property would not taint the fourteen-day tax-free rental rule because that tax loophole pertains specifically to Brandon's primary home. The new property would be treated just like any other rental property, and when it comes to short-term rentals, there are actually two possible treatments under the IRS rules. The rental income is either taxed the same as regular rental income, or it can be taxed as active business income just like a hotel business.

As an investor, we generally want our short-term rentals to be treated just like regular long-term rentals for tax purposes. This means that we get to depreciate the property like any other residential rental real estate, and we can avoid self-employment taxes. Many investors are shocked to learn that operating rentals as an active business can actually result in additional self-employment taxes of up to 15 percent. Here is an example of the tax difference between treating a property as a rental business versus an active business:

	Rental Business	Active Business
Rental Income	$25,000	$25,000
Rental Expenses	($2,000)	($2,000)
Net Taxable Rental Income	$23,000	$23,000
Income Taxes @ 24%	$5,520	$5,520
Self-Employment Taxes @ 15%	—	$3,450
Total Taxes	$5,520	$8,970

In our example, operating the rental as an active business versus rental business can result in an additional $3,450 in total taxes owed to the IRS.

Rental Business Versus Active Business

What exactly is the difference between a rental business and an active business? First, it has nothing to do with how the property title is held. It does not matter whether the title to the property is held in the investor's personal name or in an entity name. The distinction is also not impacted by the investor's claim to be a real estate professional.

In determining whether a short-term rental should be reported as regular rental income or as active business income, the IRS looks to the "services" provided for the guests. If "substantial services" are provided to the guests, the property would be treated as active real estate income and would thus be subject to the additional 15 percent self-employment tax.

An example of such a service could be daily cleaning. If you—or a crew you hire—go clean up the place every day, that might be indicative of providing substantial services. On the other hand, if you or your crew simply go in to clean up the property after one set of guests leave and before the next guests arrive, that would generally not turn your short-term rental income into an active business. Here are some other common examples of substantial services:

- Transportation services, such as airport pickup and drop-off
- Daily cleaning, laundry, or linen services
- Concierge types of services
- Providing food and beverage
- Conducting tours or other outings and events
- Other "hotel-type" services

As you can see, most of these activities are usually provided by hotels and generally not by short-term rental operators on platforms such as Airbnb and Vrbo. If you do not provide these types of services, the rental income from your short-term rentals would generally be taxed the same as your regular long-term rentals.

As a short-term operator, what type of services can you provide that can still help you remain a regular rental business? If you provide internet services or cable TV to your tenants, would that put you in the active business category? Although hotels do provide internet and cable, offering these items to your guests does not automatically mean you now need to pay higher taxes like hotels do. Here are some common examples that can generally be provided by short-term rental investors who could still be considered a regular rental business:

- Water, gas, heating, cooling, and other utilities
- Furnished units
- Cleaning of common areas
- Cable, internet, and Wi-Fi

- Incidental supplies such as bottled water, salt and pepper, toilet paper, soap

As such, we rarely come across a short-term rental investor who falls into the "active business" definition that results in the need to pay additional taxes. In other words, most short-term investors receive the same tax benefits as long-term rental investors and also receive higher cash flow. With the higher cash flow comes the need for additional planning in order to reduce or eliminate the taxes on the rental income.

Short-term rental investors receive all the same tax benefits as traditional long-term rental investors, which means that investors can write off business-related expenses such as repair costs, mortgage interest, home office, business meals, and travel—just to name a few. For example, if you had a rental property by the beach, driving to the beach property to meet with a prospective tenant is a legitimate tax deduction. If you decided to stay at an Airbnb owned by one of your competitors so that you could see what things you can improve on for your own rental, that might also be a legitimate tax deduction.

Oftentimes an investor may rent out their primary home or portions of their home as a short-term rental as well. Maximizing tax deductions for a property that is partially personal and partially a rental property can be a little tricky. If a property is both personal and a rental, it is considered a mixed-use property. This can either be treated as personal use property, a rental property, or a dwelling unit used as a home—and there are different tax treatments for each of these three scenarios. The treatment will depend on the specifics of how often the property is rented, which portion of the property would be rented, and the rental arrangement.

Personal Use Property

A personal use property is defined as a home that you use or live in for more than fourteen days out of the year. In addition, the property must have been rented out for less than fifteen days. A perfect example would be Brandon; he lived in his apartment all year and he only rented it out for less than fifteen days. The personal use property is beneficial because the rental income is tax-free, and you get to claim a personal deduction for 100 percent of the mortgage interest and property taxes of your home as your primary residence. This is the best of both worlds.

Rental Property

A rental property is defined when the number of personal-use days does not exceed either fourteen days or 10 percent of the rental days, whichever is greater. For tax purposes, the property is shown both as a rental and as a personal home. This means that you would prorate the expenses between personal and rental use. Therefore, for mortgage interest and property taxes, a portion would be deductible against the rental income and a portion would still be deductible as a personal itemized deduction for your primary residence as usual. For other indirect expenses that benefit the entire house, such as utilities or maintenance, a portion would be deductible against the rental income. The personal-use portion would be considered a non-deductible personal expense. However, for any expenses directly related to the rental, such as advertising or linens and supplies, the entire amount would be deducted against the rental income.

Dwelling Unit Used as a Home

The third scenario of a mixed-use property is referred to as a dwelling unit used as a home. This applies to a home that you use or live in for more than fourteen days out of the year or 10 percent of the rental days, whichever is greater. Plus, you must rent out the property for more than fourteen days, because remember: If you rent out a property for fewer than fourteen days, the income does not need to be reported!

As with the rental property above, you would prorate expenses between personal and rental use. This means that you would be able to deduct the personal portion of mortgage interest and real estate taxes as part of personal deductions on Schedule A. The prorated interest and taxes with respect to the rental portion would be deductible against rental income. In addition, any expenses directly related to the rental, such as advertising or linens and supplies, could be deducted against the rental income.

However, for indirect expenses that benefit the entire house, there is a hidden trap. These other indirect operating expenses of the rental property can only reduce rental income down to zero and cannot create a loss. For example, if the property had rental income of $2,000, allocated interest and tax expense of $1,500, and other indirect operational expenses of $1,700. The calculation would be as follows:

Rental income: $2,000

Interest and taxes: −$1,500

Other expenses: −$500 (Limited by rental income)

Total rental income: $0

As you can see, even though we had other indirect rental expenses of $1,700, only $500 could have been used in that year because—for properties that are considered to be a dwelling unit used as a home—indirect operational and maintenance expenses could not create a net rental loss for that property. The good news, though, is that the unallowed losses are not lost forever. They are just carried forward into subsequent years to offset future rental income.

As you can see, mixed-use properties can be a bit confusing from a tax perspective. We have created a flowchart in Appendix D to help you determine which treatment a particular property might fall under.

For properties that are purely short-term rentals, the tax treatment is much simpler. Effectively, all expenses would be deductible against rental income and you do not need to worry about prorating any expenses. As indicated previously, when income increases significantly, more planning may be needed in order to reduce taxes from that income. As such, capturing the expenses correctly for the short-term rental becomes extremely important.

As a short-term rental operator, it is common to incur overhead expenses such as bottled water, coffee, cream, salt and pepper, and other condiments. These items should be classified as supplies and expensed in the year purchased. Although most business meals are subject to a 50 percent deduction limitation, these items would generally not fall under that limitation because they are treated as supplies and incidentals.

We often see investors operate multiple short-term rentals. If you go to Costco and purchase toilet paper and other supplies in bulk that are later used across multiple rental properties, you can either deduct them as part of overall rental expenses or you can use any reasonable method to allocate them among the different properties. For the most part, a net rental loss from one short-term property can generally be used to offset the rental income from another short-term rental, or vice versa. If you have a lot of passive loss carryforwards, it might make sense to turn some of your long-term rentals into short-term rentals so that you can have increased cash flow that would be tax-free after applying your other passive losses against them.

Another great way to reduce taxable income from short-term rentals is with accelerated depreciation. It is not uncommon for investors to fully furnish the property before placing it in service as a short-term rental. Common assets for short-term rentals include various furniture and fixtures for the property. Many investors also supply appliances such as washing machines, dryers, dishwashers, coffee machines, and gaming consoles. These items are all eligible for depreciation and may even be eligible for such special treatment as bonus depreciation or Section 179 immediate expensing. Under certain circumstances, an investor might also be able to make a *de minimis* safe harbor election , which allows the investor to take an immediate expense for items that cost under $2,500, like furniture, fixtures, and appliances. These can add up to some pretty significant amounts, especially in the first year of operation.

Besides accelerating the depreciation on furniture and appliances, cost segregation is also a great potential strategy to reduce taxes from short-term rentals. In fact, cost segregation might potentially wipe out all the taxable income from the rental property for several years into the future.

Dee operates a short-term rental business. She has three rental properties near the lake and has been renting them out on Airbnb for the past six months. Because of the great reviews she has received, Dee's properties are generally rented out as soon as a date opens up. She is expecting to make close to $120,000 of rental income just from these three properties. If she uses the correct tax strategies, Dee might be able to pay zero taxes on her rental income for that year:

Dee's Airbnb	
Rental Income	$120,000
Operational Expenses	($25,000)
Interest & Taxes	($18,000)
Accelerated Depreciation	($95,000)
Net Tax Loss	**($18,000)**

In addition to paying no taxes on her rental income, Dee finds she is also able to create a net loss of $18,000 from these three short-term rentals. That loss can be used to offset taxes from other sources or carried forward to offset next year's rental income from those lake properties and from other rental properties. By not having to pay any taxes on her rental income, Dee is able to keep all her profits, which results in more money that she can use to buy more rentals.

Rental Arbitrage

Generating cash flow from short-term rentals is not a strategy limited to property owners. This strategy can also be used either for those who don't have enough money to purchase a property or for those who simply do not want to own a property. The strategy is commonly referred to as rental arbitrage; it involves an investor renting a property from the property owner and then subleasing it out to guests on a short-term basis. The arbitrage represents the profits made from the price difference between the rental income (earned from the short-term guests) minus the rent that the investor pays to the landlord (for the long-term rent). For example, if you rented a home and paid the landlord $1,000 per month and then subleased that home on a short-term basis to generate rental income of $2,500, you would have a profit from rental arbitrage of $1,500 per month.

From a tax perspective, income from rental arbitrage is treated the same as regular long-term rentals. The only major tax difference between rental arbitrage and regular short-term rentals is depreciation. For rental arbitrage investors, there is no depreciation deduction on the rental property itself because the investor does not own the property. As such, depreciation is taken by the property owner, the landlord. As an investor involved in rental arbitrage, however, you are able to deduct the rent expense paid to the landlord. This may not be a bad trade-off, especially since the entire rent expense may be tax-deductible, and you also do not need to worry about any depreciation recapture. Of course, if you provide furniture, fixtures, and appliances, those items can be depreciated to reduce rental income as well.

As with other short-term rentals, the income would generally be treated like regular rental income if there were not any significant services offered for the property, such as daily cleaning, food and beverage, and transportation. If hotel-type services are offered, then the activity would be considered active income and be subject to self-employment taxes in addition to federal and state income taxes.

Operating a Hotel

Although the vast majority of short-term rental operators on platforms such as Airbnb and Vrbo do not provide hotel-type services, there are investors who strategically do provide additional services in order to stand out from the crowd and potentially charge a higher amount of rent. Even though that type of income may be subject to additional self-employment taxes of up to 15 percent, does that mean you shouldn't consider it as a valid strategy? After all, there are bound to be tax strategies for real estate investors no matter how you earn your money, right?

If you find yourself providing hotel-type services for your short-term rentals, all hope is not lost as it relates to taxes. As discussed earlier, you can use all of the same rental strategies that are used by traditional landlords, such as deducting your real estate expenses and maximizing depreciation. If, after using the traditional strategies, there is still a significant amount of taxable income left, one way to potentially reduce the taxes on that income might be with retirement planning.

Let's change the facts for Dee and assume that she does not own her rental property and is instead using the rental arbitrage strategy. In order to maximize her rental income, Dee also has the option of having her guests pay her additional money for airport pickup and drop-off. If desired, the guests can also pay a fee for Dee to provide daily cleaning for the property, as well as delivery and cleanup of meals. Because Dee does not own the property, there is no depreciation expense. Since she provides hotel-type services, this rental is considered an active income business and subject to income and self-employment taxes. Using a retirement planning strategy, Dee can still lower her taxes as follows:

Dee's Airbnb Hotel	
Rental Income	$65,000
Operational Expenses	($46,000)
Depreciation	—
Net Tax Income	$19,000
Retirement Contribution	($19,000)
Taxable Income	—

In our example, Dee is able to use a Solo 401(k) to completely wipe out her rental income from income taxes. This account is an individual 401(k) for the self-employed and the business owner who has no employees. As you can see, one of the benefits of operating a short-term rental as an active business is the ability to redistribute tax dollars that would otherwise go to the IRS into retirement accounts. This is a great benefit that is typically not available for rental income because most rental income is not eligible for retirement contribution purposes. Dee's rental income is eligible for retirement contributions because it is taxed as active income and subject to self-employment taxes.

If Dee sets up her Solo 401(k) as a self-directed retirement account, not only will she have reduced taxes on $19,000 of rental income, but she will be able to reinvest that $19,000 into other real estate deals as well.

Another important aspect to note is that the tax treatment of your short-term rental is on a property-by-property basis. This means that Dee can have a property that is completely tax-free because it is her home that was rented out for fourteen days or less during the year. She can also have a duplex where one unit is a long-term rental and another unit is a short-term rental. She can also use rental arbitrage on other real estate to generate cash flow. The tax treatment for each of those will be unique, depending on how the property was operated during that year.

Many investors are interested in turning their properties into short-term rentals but don't know where to start. Others may be hesitant to get into short-term rentals because they are afraid it would take up too much of their time and turn into a full-time job. Just as with any real estate or business, it is important to create systems around what you do. Systems can be put in place on the marketing, booking, collection, cleanup, and stocking of the properties. As an investor, you do not necessarily need to spend countless hours managing or operating short-term rentals. If this is something that may be applicable to any of your existing or future properties, the additional cash may be worth the time to give this investment strategy some thought.

WHAT DOES IT ALL MEAN?

Short-term rentals are usually treated the same as long-term rentals for tax purposes. Investors can take write-offs and depreciation to offset the rental income. A wonderful loophole exists when you rent out your home as a short-term rental for fewer than fifteen days during the year. In those instances, the rental income may be completely tax-free, and you still retain the right to deduct your entire mortgage interest and property taxes if this is your primary home. For mixed-use properties that are part-personal use and part-rental use, there may be proration calculations required for the expenses and certain deductions may be limited to rental income.

For short-term rentals that include hotel-type services, additional self-employment taxes may be assessed. But the silver lining for those types of short-term rentals is that retirement contribution strategies may be used to reduce the taxes from that active income.

CHAPTER 6
A TALE OF TWO INVESTORS: FLIP VS. BRRRR

"If you don't know where you are going, you'll end up someplace else."

—YOGI BERRA

Growing up, Tom and Jim spent their summer breaks watching all those house-flipping shows on TV; spending the summer by tackling their first real estate investment together sounded like a ton of fun. Adults now, they felt ready for the challenge and were excited for all the things they might learn along the way. Who knew? Maybe they would get famous and be invited to have their own reality TV show on house flipping.

As first-time investors, Tom and Jim wanted their first deal to be somewhat close to home. They both knew they wanted to work on smaller single-family properties with around three bedrooms and two bathrooms, and nothing that would require an extensive rehab. They had seen plenty of remodels that had gone wrong, and they had a very limited amount of cash on hand. Since most of the cash they had would be used to purchase the property, they planned to do all the rehab work themselves.

Tom and Jim knew that the first step was to find a great deal. They had been attending a local real estate investors' group for a few weeks, and there they met Sharon, a full-time accountant. Her father had left her a few rental properties through his living trust that she wanted to sell. They included two smaller properties next door to each other that had had the same tenants in them for over the last decade. They were paying under-market rent, and the place desperately needed a face-lift. Each was a 2-bedroom, 1-bathroom house with a detached garage. According to Sharon, each property could likely see an increase of about $50,000 in value after putting in $20,000 of improvements.

The very next day, Tom and Jim met Sharon at the two rental properties. In addition to paint and flooring, they would also need to update the fixtures of each house. An update of the cabinets and countertops, as well as some new appliances, would give the kitchen a completely modern look. None of that seemed too complicated because they would not need to change the footprint of the house.

After the property tour, Tom and Jim were excited to get started on this deal. As an accountant, Sharon had a tip for them: Instead of the two of them purchasing both properties together, it might make more sense for each to purchase one rental. That way, if Tom and Jim had different exit strategies for the properties once the rehab was done, then they could each make their own decision more easily without impacting the other too much. They agreed with Sharon that each would buy a property on their own. With their competitive nature, they could even make this more interesting by seeing who could make more money on their first flip.

Before finalizing the deal, Sharon had another tip for Tom and Jim: Don't forget about Uncle Sam. Sharon reminded them that taxes would need to be paid on the profit from the flip. Before going out and spending all that profit or reinvesting it all into their next flip deal, they should make sure to set money aside for taxes when the time came.

Immediately after closing on the properties, Tom and Jim each jumped right into demolition mode. They spent two days ripping out the old flooring and cabinets and began the design process. Over the next few weeks, they chugged along on the rehab work. Working longer than ten-hour days and often on the weekends, they were a little surprised to find that things took a little longer than what they had originally expected. Fortunately for Tom and Jim, the longer rehab time actually turned out to be a blessing in disguise. A sudden drop in interest rates created a buying frenzy, and several other properties in the neighborhood sold for great prices. If things went well, Tom and Jim would each be looking at a profit of close to $80,000 on the sale of the properties.

Tom and Jim decided to ask Sharon to join them for lunch to catch up on the project. Considering the larger-than-expected profit of $80,000 for each of them, Sharon shared some not-so-great news: The taxes could be as high as 50 percent.

Until now, this was the only income they had made that year. How was it possible that their tax rate would go as high as more than 50 percent? It seemed impossible to them. What about all the benefits for being real estate investors they had always heard about? Would those not help them pay lower taxes?

Sharon explained that fix-and-flip profit was different from rental real state investing. When it comes to taxes, Sharon explained, flip profit is treated as ordinary income. In other words, flipping real estate is the same as if you had opened a burger shop and flipped hamburgers. She described how flipping properties has two major downsides:

- Flip profit is subject to ordinary income tax rates and not the lower capital gains tax rates
- Flip profit is subject not only to federal and state income taxes, but to self-employment taxes as well

With the example of Tom's property, Sharon scribbled this calculation on the back of her napkin:

Example of Taxes on Tom's Flip	
Property Sale Price	**$175,000** A
Property Purchase Price	($80,000)
Total Rehab Costs	($15,000)
Total Cost Basis	**($95,000)**
Net Flip Profit	**$80,000**
Federal Income Taxes @ 22%	$17,600
State Income Taxes @ 10%	$8,000
Self-Employment Taxes @ 15%	$12,000
Total Taxes @ 47%	**$37,600** B
Net Cash After Taxes (A − B)	**$137,400**

According to Sharon's rough estimate, after factoring in federal income taxes, state income taxes, and self-employment taxes, Tom would need to pay the IRS and state more than $37,000 in taxes on the sale of the flip property—a total tax cost of roughly 47 percent. To Tom, losing close to half of his flip profit to the government was just not acceptable. There had to be another way.

Sharon offered up another solution: Instead of selling the property right then as a flip, maybe they could consider holding on to the property as a rental. By doing so, they might be able to lower their taxes or even defer the tax to many years down the road. The difference, according to Sharon, could mean paying $37,000 in taxes or paying zero taxes that year.

Jim didn't love the idea. His plan all along had been to sell the property so he could take the cash to do another flip. Even if he paid the taxes on that, he would still have more money for his next deal than what he had started with that summer. Jim was familiar with the saying "There are two certainties in life—death and taxes." To him, paying taxes was simply another cost of doing business. He did not feel it made sense to keep the property as a rental. After all, his entire life savings was tied up in the deal. If he kept the property as a rental, the most he could get would be $1,100 in rent each month, and after expenses, there might not be much left.

In Jim's mind, the only way for him to get to the next flip deal was to sell this property, and soon. In fact, it was time for him to leave lunch to meet with a potential buyer. Even though the property was not yet listed for sale, a neighbor had approached Jim just a week prior because she was interested in buying the property and insisted on being the first to see it.

Jim thanked Sharon for her time and left the meeting in a hurry. Tom explained to her that, although it sounded nice that they would be able to pay lower taxes, it might not really be an option for them because their plan all along was to use the profit from the flip. If only there was a way to get money out of this property and into the next deal without paying taxes.

"What if I told you there *was* a way to have both?" Sharon asked. With Tom's full attention, she told him that he could turn the flip into a "BRRRR" property.

From Broke to BRRRR

BRRRR is an acronym that represents the five stages of what can be an extremely lucrative real estate investing strategy. (Needless to say, this is an oversimplified version of the process. To learn more about the BRRRR strategy, check out the book *Buy, Rehab, Rent, Refinance, Repeat* by David Greene.)

The five stages are as follows:

Buy

The buy step is just what it sounds like: purchasing a property. In order for the investor to successfully use the BRRRR strategy, it must be an undervalued property so that renovations can be done to create forced appreciation. As an example, a property purchased from a turnkey provider is typically not going to be great for the BRRRR strategy, because that property is already in its highest and best use when it was purchased. Tom's property was purchased under value, so step one was covered.

Rehab

Step two is to rehab the property. Although renovating the property is likely the first thing that comes to mind when we talk about rehabbing, it doesn't necessarily need end there. Rehabbing can also mean changing the property to its highest and best use from other activities, such as adding square footage, changing the footprint of the property, or changing the use of the property (for instance, changing it from residential to commercial or from a single unit to multiple units). Essentially, the goal in this process is to create forced appreciation so that after the rehab is done, the property is worth more than the sum of what you purchased it for plus the cost of the improvements you made. At this point, the Buy and Rehab steps matched up exactly with what Tom had already done on his flip deal.

Rent

The next R represents rent. Before renting it out, you should analyze the property to see how it would perform as a rental property. At the end of the day, keeping the property must make financial sense before the decision is made to turn a flip into a rental. Tom had not really thought about that before because all along, he and Jim had planned on flipping the properties. However, based on what Tom knew of the surrounding areas, the newly rehabbed property could easily generate a good return. Especially since so much work was just recently done to the house, there was little to no deferred maintenance left to be done, so it should have been a fairly hassle-free property to hold on to as long as he could find good tenants.

Refinance

Once the property is rented out, the next step in the BRRRR process is to refinance. This is a key part of the transaction that could potentially help Tom achieve his original goal of getting into more deals. Remember that Tom had planned on selling the property in order to get cash to use in his next deal? Well, instead of selling the property to get the cash, Tom could instead look at refinancing the property to pull the cash out. While many investors refinance to get a better rate and terms or to lower their monthly payments, refinancing can also allow an investor to get money out of the deal. If a refinance could be done on this property, it just might be the solution to his tax problems.

Repeat

If the strategy is implemented correctly, BRRRR allows you to buy a property, rehab it to increase the value, take cash out of the deal by doing a refinance, and then use that cash to get started on your next deal. As you can see, these steps can be repeated over and over again to allow you to buy more cash-flowing properties without the need to sell any of them.

This all sounded feasible to Tom. It was definitely different from his original plan of selling the property immediately. Even though he could get some positive cash flow by keeping the property and get cash out of the deal by refinancing, there would still be the process of finding tenants and filling out the paperwork to obtain a loan. And if Tom was to be honest with himself, he wasn't sure he was ready to be a landlord. Before Tom could make a decision, he needed to know what the tax impact would be. How much would he actually save in taxes?

The Taxes Behind BRRRR

According to Sharon, turning the property from a flip into a BRRRR could help Tom defer some of his taxes into future years and also eliminate part of his taxes permanently. Here's why:

No taxes are due at the present on the property appreciation

If Tom were to sell the property as a flip this year, he would have to pay federal, state, and self-employment taxes of up to a combined 47 percent rate, which would end up being $37,600 in actual tax dollars. Alternatively, if he were to turn the property into a rental, then he would pay zero taxes that year. Tom would not be taxed on the appreciation of the property until the property was sold. Even though the property was then worth $175,000, and his cost basis was $95,000, the appreciation of $80,000 did not result in any taxable income in the current year. That gain would generally be taxed in the year Tom decided to sell the property.

No taxes are due at the present on the refinance proceeds

With the property value at $175,000, Tom was hoping to take out a loan at 80 percent of the value, in the amount of $140,000. With this money, he should have been able to buy his next property and have enough cash left over for rehab costs on his next project. From a tax perspective, loan proceeds from a refinance were tax-free money that Tom could access.

If Tom had sold the property, he would have ended up with $137,400 of net cash after taxes. If he kept the property, he would end up with $140,000 of cash after refinance. This meant that, by using the BRRRR strategy, Tom would actually end up with *more* cash that year than what he otherwise would have, and he would get to keep his property to earn more cash flow in the coming years.

Tax-deductible interest

There is bound to be interest expense on the new loan for refinancing the property. However, because the loan proceeds were to be used to purchase and improve another rental property, Tom could also deduct the interest expense on the new loan. The interest could offset taxes from his rental income. It was recommended that Tom trace his money carefully to show that the loan proceeds were used solely for the purchase of an additional investment property in order to ensure his interest remained tax-deductible.

Depreciation from rental property can offset taxable income

In addition to not paying taxes on the refinance proceeds and being able to deduct the interest expense, turning the flip into a BRRRR offered another great tax savings opportunity regarding depreciation. Although a flip property is not eligible for depreciation, a rental property is—and since a BRRRR property is, in essence, a rental property, it generates depreciation tax benefits. In Tom's example, he purchased the property for $80,000 and put in improvements of $15,000, which means he has $95,000 of property basis that he can calculate depreciation on.

Not only that, Tom may be able to use cost segregation to accelerate the depreciation on the rental property to create more deductions that could be used to offset his rental income or flip profit on any future potential flips. Since Tom was the one who rehabbed the property, he would be able to break out the components of his rehab work. Using the breakout details, his CPA would be able to help him accelerate the depreciation expense. For example, the money that Tom spent on the purchase of the appliances, fixtures, and cabinets may receive faster depreciation than the building itself, to help lower any taxes that would otherwise be due to the IRS.

Permanent tax savings

As Sharon indicated previously, fix-and-flip profit is generally not treated as capital gains income. Instead it is taxed as ordinary income which is subject to potentially higher income tax rates. Once a property is turned into a BRRRR property, the eventual sale of the property also turns the profit into capital gains. This means that if the property is held longer than a year, the gain on the sale can be treated as long term capital gains which can receive lower tax treatment. In Tom's example, the difference would be paying ordinary income taxes of 22 percent to the IRS vs. later paying long-term capital gains taxes at only 15 percent.

In addition to higher ordinary income tax rates, flip profit is also subject to self-employment taxes, which are paid into social security and Medicare and can be over 15 percent. Another nice thing about the BRR-RR strategy is that self-employment taxes do not apply to rental income. Turning a flip property into a BRRRR property means that you can also avoid the additional 15 percent self-employment tax that could otherwise be due when a property is sold as a flip.

Tax deferral down the road

Many investors are familiar with the ability to defer taxes using a 1031 exchange. A 1031 exchange allows the taxpayer to sell an investment property and defer paying taxes on the capital gains when they reinvest the money in another investment property.

To many, this seems like a good way to defer taxes when they sell a flip property. What many people may not know is that fix-and-flip properties are not eligible for tax deferral in a 1031 exchange. Because the IRS treats flip property like inventory, it is not considered "investment property" under IRS definitions and thus is not eligible for the tax deferral. This means that, if Tom were to sell the property as a flip property, he would not be able to defer the taxes on the capital gains, even if he uses the profits from the first flip to buy his next flip property.

A tax deferral using a 1031 exchange can, however, be used for rental properties. So, if Tom uses BRRRR to turn the current property into a rental and then decides down the road to sell this rental, he may be able to defer the taxes using a 1031 exchange provided that he will be reinvesting his money into more rental or BRRRR properties. He would not, however, be able to sell the current BRRRR property and replace that money into a flip property using a 1031 exchange. By turning the property into a rental, Tom can defer the tax into the future year when the property is sold, avoid the self-employment taxes, and pay the lower capital gains tax rates.

How Long Must the Property Be Kept as a Rental?

You may be asking yourself: *What exactly is the difference in calling a property a flip versus a BRRRR?* If you listed your property for rent on Airbnb or Vrbo and rented it out for a few weeks, would you have in essence turned your flip into a BRRRR and then be eligible for all these great tax benefits? What if you rented it out for a month to your brother and then sold it after that?

There is no clear guideline from the IRS in terms of how long you must hold a property in order for it to be a rental property. For example, there is no safe harbor that says if you hold it longer than six months then you are fine, or that if you hold it less than three months then it would not qualify. It all comes down to facts and circumstances. This means that the IRS will evaluate each situation on its own. The agency will take into the consideration the entire profile of the taxpayer along with the taxpayer's demonstrated intent with respect to the property.

Intent plays a big role if the IRS were to challenge the position of someone claiming a property to be a rental. For example, what if Tom found a tenant for his property, signed a two-year lease, but a few months after moving in the tenant stopped paying and trashed the place? And after the tenant moved out, Tom realized that he would not be able to hold on to the property with all the repairs it then needed. If he sold the property a few months later, he could have a reasonable argument that this was a rental property, as long as he could show his intent all along was to keep this property as a rental.

Sometimes there are investors who purchase rentals and later find out that the association changed its rules to then prohibit owners from renting it out. In that scenario, there was a change in facts that prevented the investor from renting out the property, so they just ended up selling due to those changes.

On the other hand, what if Tom had the property listed for sale on the MLS when he was still rehabbing the property, started showing the property to potential buyers as soon as it was completed, and then rented it out to his cousin for a month while the property was going through escrow? Claiming it as a rental property would likely be disallowed by the IRS, since his intent appeared to position the property as a flip property all along.

The IRS also looks at other activities that the investor is involved in. If, for example, Tom flipped three other properties and had a fourth property rented out for a month before selling it, it would be easier for the IRS to argue that this fourth property was also intended to be a flip. Alternatively, if Tom owned three other rentals and then needed to sell the fourth rental shortly after placing it in service due to some unexpected changes, it could potentially be easier for Tom to prove rental intent.

Same Numbers, Different Answers

Before Sharon and Tom parted for lunch, she reminded him that another benefit of the BRRRR strategy is that the BRRRR property produces depreciation expense. Often the depreciation expense can also be used to reduce taxes from any flip properties that he might sell during the year.

Tom could not wait to tell Jim about this new strategy he had learned. When they met up back at the property, he found out that when Jim had just showed the property, it had gone extremely well. Anticipating a high demand, the buyer had decided to make a great offer in order to lock up the property. Before the day was over, Jim had a signed contract for his property at $10,000 above the fair market value. It felt amazing to have a signed contract on the property before it was even listed for sale. Tom was ecstatic for Jim as well.

The bad news was that Jim would need to pay the income and self-employment taxes on his first flip. Tom did not want to rain on Jim's parade by bringing up the fact that Jim may have saved a ton in taxes had he not sold the property right away. Who knows? Maybe for Jim's next deal, he will decide to do the BRRRR strategy instead of a straight flip, and the depreciation from that new rental could be used to reduce taxes on this first flip that he sold today.

WHAT DOES IT ALL MEAN?

The U.S. tax system is full of pitfalls and hidden loopholes. Many investors do not know that flip properties are subject to much higher taxes than rental properties. There are many ways to reduce taxes on flip properties and one of those is to simply turn a flip into a rental. Once a flip property is turned into a rental, some of the possible tax benefits include:

- The ability to avoid self-employment taxes of up to 15 percent
- The ability to receive the lower long-term capital gains tax rate
- The tax benefit of having depreciation expense from the property
- The ability to potentially defer taxes down the road with a 1031 exchange

Instead of selling a rehabbed property immediately as a flip, consider whether the BRRRR method may be a better alternative. When used correctly, a BRRRR property may allow an investor to take cash out of a deal and to reinvest into more deals with little to no taxes today!

CHAPTER 7

PLAYING KEEP AWAY FROM THE IRS USING 1031 EXCHANGE

"America is a land of taxation that was founded to avoid taxation."

—DR. LAURENCE J. PETER

John and Lisa met at a real estate conference two years ago, and it was love at first sight. They both had a career in advertising and a passion for real estate investing. They bonded over success and horror stories of their experiences as landlords, and after dating for just a few months, they became a happy newlywed couple.

John owned a fourplex on Freemont Street that he had purchased about two years prior for $350,000. The property cash flowed well and had very few maintenance issues. Overall, it had been a good investment for John. A few months after coming back from their honeymoon, John and Lisa were approached by a developer who was interested in building an apartment building where John's property was. Most of the neighbors had agreed to sell their property to the developer already, and John was one of the last ones the developer had to talk to. It was a wonderful surprise to both

John and Lisa when the developer offered them $800,000 to purchase the property. The offer was too good to pass up. Their plan was to use all the proceeds from the sale of Freemont Street to buy more rental properties.

When John and Lisa came to us to tell us about this amazing offer, we were thrilled. We knew that this was not only a great real estate deal but also that it was a great situation for them from a tax perspective. Based on our calculations, they would normally be looking at capital gains taxes of over $150,000 after factoring in depreciation recapture, selling expenses, etc. However, because their plan was to reinvest the money from the sale of Freemont Street into more rental real estate, they had the opportunity to defer the $150,000 in taxes from this transaction using a 1031 exchange.

The 1031 exchange strategy would allow John and Lisa to pay zero taxes in the year of the sale of the Freemont Street property and instead invest 100 percent of their entire proceeds into additional rental properties immediately. There are several timing, money, and other requirements that need to be met in order to receive this wonderful tax deferral treatment, but if done correctly, this could be a wonderful way for John and Lisa to continue to build their real estate portfolio.

What exactly is a 1031 exchange, and how does it work? A 1031 exchange is the sale of an investment property with the subsequent purchase of one or more replacement properties, with which you can defer paying taxes on the initial sale. Assuming you meet all the various rules and requirements for a valid 1031 exchange, you would not have to pay any income taxes that would otherwise be due in the year of the sale. Those taxes are deferred down the road until the investor sells the replacement properties in a taxable transaction.

For John and Lisa, their ability to defer $150,000 in taxes meant having that additional money to invest in more properties to grow their real estate portfolio. Rather than paying the IRS $150,000 in taxes, they could instead use that money as a down payment that could eventually generate additional cash flow and appreciation.

What Properties Are Eligible for a 1031 Exchange?

The underlying premise of a 1031 exchange is that you are selling real estate property and replacing it with real estate property that is "like-kind." The property being sold must be held for "investment" or used in a trade or business. Investment property can be a rental property that you invest in to generate cash flow, or it can be a farm property that generates income from crops. It can even be a property that you hold on to solely for appreciation benefits, like raw land. Eligible property can also include an office building or a warehouse that your business has owned and used for its business operations.

Like-kind refers to the fact that you need to purchase a similar property as a replacement. It must be another investment property or another property used in your trade or business. This doesn't mean that if you sell a single-family home rental you need to replace it with another single-family home rental. You could replace it with a fourplex, a hotel, an office building, or even vacant land. Remember Monopoly, the popular game where you turn in, or "exchange," your four green houses for the one red hotel? Same concept here.

Eligible properties for a 1031 exchange can include, but aren't necessarily limited to, the following:
- Single family rental
- Duplex, triplex, or fourplex
- Apartment building
- Hotel
- Office building
- Shopping or retail center
- Triple net lease property
- Vacant land or farmland
- Tenant in common interest in real property
- Leasehold interests
- Qualified property in one state for qualified property in another state
- Domestic (U.S.) property for domestic (U.S.) property
- Foreign (Non-U.S.) property for foreign (Non-U.S.) property
- Oil and gas interests
- Mineral, water, or timber rights
- Delaware Statutory Trusts (DSTs)

As you can see, there are many options for John and Lisa in a 1031 exchange. As they shop for their replacement property, they are not limited to looking for just fourplex rentals. In fact, they could sell their fourplex and replace it with one or more of these investment properties listed above in a 1031 exchange.

What Assets or Properties Are Not Eligible for a 1031 Exchange?

Although there are a lot of different types of properties that are eligible to be sold in a 1031 exchange, there are also ineligible properties. These include the following:

- Primary residences not used as a rental
- Second/vacation homes not used as a rental
- Personal property such as furniture, fixtures, equipment, appliances
- Fix-and-flip properties
- Partnership and LLC interests
- Stock in an entity, such as a C corporation or an S corporation
- Bonds, notes or loans, securities, or certificates of trust
- Inventory or dealer properties
- Domestic (U.S.) property for foreign (Non-U.S.) property (or the other way around)

Although you can cross state lines by selling a property in one state and buying a replacement property in another, you cannot cross international lines. This means that if you sell a property located in the United States, your replacement property must be located in the United States. If you sell a non-U.S. property, you must replace it with a non-U.S. property.

As with everything in taxes, there are always exceptions to the general rules. If you are in doubt as to whether your property qualifies, always speak with your tax advisor and your 1031 exchange intermediary about your situation before starting the transaction.

What Are the Time Requirements?

In addition to purchasing like-kind replacement property, there are essentially two different time requirements that you need to meet in order to receive the tax benefit of a 1031 exchange.

45-Day Deadline to Identify Replacement Properties

The first time requirement is the 45-Day Identification Deadline. This rule states that, within 45 days after the close of the sale of your "old" or "relinquished" property, you must identify in writing, to your intermediary, a list of potential replacement properties that you are interested in purchasing.

The 45 days is based on calendar days and not weekdays. This also doesn't skip holidays. If a holiday falls within your 45-day period, then it's counted as one of your 45 days. For example, if your property sold on March 1, your list of replacement properties must be identified and submitted to your intermediary by April 15, which is 45 calendar days after March 1. This date is extremely important, as you are required to disclose it on your tax return when you report your exchange, so make sure you don't miss it.

What many investors do not know is that the IRS requires you to submit your list of potential replacement properties to your intermediary in writing. This should not be done over a phone call or verbally in a face-to-face meeting. You should submit your written list in person, via email, fax, or regular mail. If you are going to have it delivered in person, then your intermediary will need to have it in their hands by midnight of the forty-fifth day. If you are going to mail the form to the intermediary, it needs to be postmarked by the forty-fifth day. Most good intermediaries already have a form they will give you to list your identified properties; you should fill that out and return it to them by the deadline.

HOW MANY PROPERTIES DO I NEED TO IDENTIFY?

This one is simple. You need to identify at least one potential replacement property that you are planning to purchase in the exchange. Although you only need to identify one, you may want to identify more than one property that meets your investing requirements, because what if your one property purchase falls through? If that happens and you do not have another potential property identified within the 45-day time frame, your entire exchange would fail and you could end up paying taxes on the entire gain of the property you sold.

HOW MANY PROPERTIES CAN I IDENTIFY?

The IRS generally allows you to identify up to a maximum of three properties in a 1031 exchange. However, you are allowed to identify more than three properties as long as the total purchase price of all the identified potential replacement properties does not exceed 200 percent of the sales price of your relinquished property. In John and Lisa's example, they sold their property for $800,000. They can identify up to three properties, regardless of the total purchase price; if they identified three replacement properties that had a total purchase price of $2 million, that would be fine.

Alternatively, if John and Lisa wanted to identify more than three properties, then the total purchase price of the identified potential replacement properties cannot exceed 200 percent of the $800,000 sales price of their duplex. If John and Lisa wanted to identify five potential replacement properties, they could submit this list of five potential replacement properties to their intermediary, as long as the total expected purchase price of the five properties did not exceed $1.6 million. This rule was designed by the IRS to prevent investors from simply listing as many potential properties as possible in a 1031 exchange.

WHAT PROPERTY INFORMATION IS NEEDED IN THE IDENTIFICATION PROCESS?

What property information do you need to provide to your intermediary within the 45-day time frame in order to meet this requirement? The information provided should be either the property's specific address or the property's legal description if it doesn't have an actual address. If you are planning to purchase a specific unit in a condo complex, office building, or shopping center, then make sure the unit number or suite number is also listed on your identification form. Obviously this also means that your identified replacement property cannot simply be a vague description like "a single-family house on Smith Ave. in San Francisco, CA" or "any property for sale in Austin, TX."

DO I NEED TO BUY ALL THE PROPERTIES IDENTIFIED ON MY LIST?

The answer is no. You do not need to purchase all the properties that you identify. The list is basically a list of properties that you are *interested* in buying. As you can see, one of the benefits of the list is that if one replacement property falls through and you identified others, you can still purchase one of the other identified properties and keep your tax deferred exchange in place. Accordingly, if you identified three properties but were only planning to purchase one of them, you can certainly do that and are not required to purchase any of the other identified properties on your list.

180-Day Purchase Deadline

The other time requirement involved in a 1031 exchange is the 180-Day Purchase Deadline, which states that you must close on the purchase of your replacement property (or properties) within 180 days after the closing date for the sale of your relinquished property. The 180-day requirement is also based on calendar days and not just weekdays. It is also not extended if a holiday falls within this period of time or even if a holiday falls on the 180th day. And similar to the 45-day requirement, the IRS does not allow for extensions to this deadline.

For example, if the sale of your relinquished property closed on Saturday, June 28, your 180-day deadline will be December 25. Yes, Christmas Day! In that case, you better make sure you close on your replacement property before that date if your escrow or title company won't be working that day.

If you are selling one property and buying one replacement property, the 180-day deadline is pretty easy to decipher. But what if you sold more than one property? If you are selling more than one property in the same like-kind exchange, then your 180-day purchase deadline clock starts on the day after the first property is sold. For example, John is planning to sell two properties in the same like-kind exchange. He sells Rental #1 on March 1 and then sells Rental #2 on June 15. The clock for the 180-day purchase deadline for his replacement properties starts on March 2, when his first rental is sold.

What if you are buying more than one replacement property? If you are purchasing more than one property in the same like-kind exchange, then your 180-day purchase deadline clock ends after all replacement properties are purchased. What does this mean? This means that you need to close on the purchase of *all* your replacement properties by day number 180. For example, John sells his fourplex on February 1 and is planning to purchase three duplexes as his replacement properties for the 1031 exchange. He closes on the purchase of Duplex #1 on June 1 and closes on the purchase of Duplex #2 on June 15. In order to fully meet his 1031 exchange requirements, he must close on the purchase of Duplex #3 by July 31, which is 180 days after February 1.

Time Requirements Can Be Stressful

As you can see from the above, the ticking 45-day and 180-day clocks can be very stressful for an investor. If you were in John and Lisa's shoes where you were facing a tax bill of up to $150,000, you obviously might want to do everything you could, legally, to keep your hard-earned money from the IRS. But what if you are on day #40 and haven't yet found a suitable replacement property where the numbers pencil out for a good deal?

You don't want to make a bad purchase just to complete the exchange. What if you have only five days left to find the right property to identify that you are going to purchase? Or what if you only have two more days until your 180-day deadline runs out but there are other things holding you up from closing on the replacement property? Sometimes getting involved in a bad deal can cost you more than the taxes that you save. This can absolutely be stressful and is something that happens more often than you may think. Thankfully, there are some suggested workarounds.

Reverse 1031 Exchange

Instead of a typical exchange in which you sell your relinquished property first and then purchase your replacement property, a "reverse exchange" involves purchasing your replacement property (or properties) before you have sold your existing property. A reverse exchange can work really well in a hot real estate market. If you feel it might take you a while to find good performing replacement properties, it could make sense to get your replacement properties under contract first before listing your current property for sale. This works especially well in a seller's market where you expect your listed property to be sold fairly quickly. Although the 45- and 180-day timelines still exist in a reverse 1031 exchange, by having the replacement properties already identified or purchased, you alleviate a lot of the time stress associated with a regular 1031 exchange.

With a reverse 1031 exchange there could be financing hurdles to take into consideration. For example, how will you purchase a replacement property if your intermediary doesn't have the funds yet from the sale of your existing property? In addition, there are also titling hurdles you may need to overcome. These hurdles can often be easily surmounted by planning proactively with your tax advisor and working with a good qualified 1031 exchange intermediary.

WHAT IF I DON'T MEET ONE OF THE 45-DAY OR 180-DAY DEADLINES?

As previously mentioned, the 45-day and 180-day deadlines are set in stone under the tax law, which means that they cannot be changed. You, as the taxpayer, can't change them. Your escrow or title company can't change them. Your lender can't change them. There are no extensions allowed by the IRS. If you don't meet the requirements for the 45-day identification deadline, then you have failed the 1031 exchange. This means the sale of your relinquished property will be treated as a normal taxable sale just like any other property sale.

What if you don't meet the 180-day purchase deadline? The tax impact in this situation can vary. If you only identified one property in the exchange and did not close on that property within the 180-day deadline, then you would have failed the exchange. In that scenario, you will pay taxes on the sale of your relinquished property the same as a normal taxable sale. However, if you identified multiple properties and closed on some but not all of them by the 180th day, it doesn't necessarily mean your entire exchange is toast. Depending on your numbers, some part of your gain on the sale of your relinquished property may still be deferred and some of it may be taxable. Again, this is where working closely with a good qualified intermediary and tax specialist will come in handy in helping to mitigate or avoid surprises like this.

What Are the Monetary Requirements?

In order to defer all the gain for tax purposes from your 1031 exchange, there are two essential monetary target amounts you must meet. The replacement properties must equal or exceed your relinquished property in both sales price and equity. Let's go over the details of each of these two requirements.

Purchase Price Target for Replacement Property

The first monetary requirement is that the total net purchase price of all your replacement properties in the exchange must equal or exceed the net sales price of your relinquished properties. For example, since John and Lisa sold their fourplex for $800,000 and were planning to purchase one replacement property, the purchase price of that property generally must be $800,000 or more.

Instead, let's say they sold the property for $800,000 on March 1 and are going to purchase multiple replacement properties by the 180-day deadline of August 28. On June 1, John and Lisa close on replacement property #1 for a purchase price of $300,000. Then on July 15, they purchase a second replacement property for $400,000. This would mean that they would need to buy one or more properties for at least $100,000 by August 28 in order to defer all the gain from the sale of their old property.

Keep in mind that selling costs and closing costs on the purchase can generally reduce these target amounts. If John and Lisa sold the property for $800,000, and their selling costs from the closing document equaled $40,000, their net sales price for the purchase price replacement target would be only $760,000.

This works the same way on the purchase side, too. You get to add your purchase closing costs to the purchase price to determine if you meet the purchase price replacement target amount. In the example below, John and Lisa must meet or exceed $760,000 as their target replacement amount—so if the replacement property they purchased costs $700,000 and the closing costs from the purchase side were at least $60,000, then they would have met or exceeded their $760,000 purchase price replacement target.

Sold Property #1		Replacement Property #2	
$800,000	Sales Price	$700,000	Purchase Price
($40,000)	Selling Costs	$60,000	Purchase Costs
$760,000	**Purchase Price Target Needed**	$760,000	**Actual Net Purchase Price**

This is another area where working closely with your team of advisors will be essential because not all closing costs listed on the sale or purchase documents count toward these calculations. Some of the costs you incur during closing are not qualified exchange costs, so planning ahead with your tax advisor before closing is crucial to making sure you are going to meet your target amounts.

Equity Target for Replacement Property

The second of the monetary replacement target requirement is that the total amount of cash (that is, the net equity) you fund into your replacement property must equal or exceed the net equity you receive from the relinquished or sold properties.

For these purposes, "net equity" or "equity" is simply referring to the following:

Sold Property	Replacement Property
Sales Price	Purchase Price
Less: Selling Costs	Plus: Purchase Closing Costs
Less: Mortgage Principle Paid Off @ Sale	Less: New Loan Balance
Equals: Net Equity	Equals: Net Equity

Essentially, this 1031 exchange rule is designed to make sure that you reinvest all the proceeds you would have received in a normal sale and that you haven't walked away with any cash from the transaction.

WHAT IF I DON'T MEET ONE OF THE MONETARY REPLACEMENT TARGETS?

As mentioned, you need to meet *both* of the monetary replacement target amounts to defer all the taxes from the gain on sale of your relinquished properties. And if you don't meet one of the requirements? Or if you don't meet both requirements? In either scenario, it does not mean your entire exchange becomes fully taxable. It simply means that you'll have to pay taxes on the amount of the shortfall. In the tax world, this shortfall is commonly referred to as "boot."

Keep in mind that the amount of income you recognize as a result of boot can never be more than the amount of the gain you would have recognized on the sale of your relinquished properties if you didn't do the exchange at all.

For example, Anthony owns Property #1 that he originally purchased five years ago for $300,000. He has taken $50,000 of depreciation expense on the property over the past five years. He sells the property for $500,000. At the time of the sale, he incurs $35,000 in selling costs and pays off the outstanding principal on the mortgage of $200,000.

If Anthony did not do a 1031 exchange, the gain on the sale of Property #1 would have looked like this:

Gain on Sale Without 1031 Exchange

$300,000	Original Purchase Price
($50,000)	Less: Accumulated Depreciation
$250,000	Adjusted Tax Basis on the Date of the Sale
$500,000	Sales Price
($35,000)	Less: Selling Costs
($250,000)	Less: Adjusted Tax Basis
$215,000	Gain on Sale of the Property

Based on a discussion with his CPA, Anthony decided to pursue a 1031 exchange to defer his taxes. This seemed to be a good strategy because he was planning to reinvest the money into additional investment properties anyway. After looking at several properties, he purchased Property #2 as his replacement property. The final purchase price of Property #2, agreed upon between Anthony and the seller, was $495,000. His total purchase costs were $25,000, and the mortgage he took out on the property is $295,000. In this scenario, did Anthony meet his monetary requirements for 1031 exchange purposes? Let's take a look.

First, let's go through the numbers to see if Anthony met the purchase price target for his replacement property:

Sold Property #1		Replacement Property #2	
$500,000	Sales Price	$495,000	Purchase Price
($35,000)	Selling Costs	$25,000	Purchase
$465,000	**Purchase Price Target Needed**	**$520,000**	**Actual Net Purchase Price**

Since the actual gross purchase price of the replacement property of $495,000 was higher than the net sales price of the sold property of $465,000, Anthony met the purchase price target for the 1031 exchange. Next let's go through the numbers to see if Anthony met the equity target for his replacement property:

Sold Property #1		Replacement Property #2	
$500,000	Sales Price	$495,000	Purchase Price
($35,000)	Selling Costs	$25,000	Purchase Costs
($200,000)	Loan Payoff at Sale	($295,000)	New Loan Balance
$265,000	**Net Equity Target Needed**	**$225,000**	**Actual Net Equity**

In this example, Anthony did not meet his equity target because his replacement property's net equity of $225,000 was less than his equity in his relinquished property of $265,000. The shortfall of $40,000 simply became taxable. As such, Anthony would pay taxes and include $40,000 of his gain on sale on his tax return. It is important to note that Anthony did not need to pay taxes on the entire $215,000 of the gain from the sale of the property. Although Anthony fell short on one of the monetary requirements, he was still able to receive a pretty substantial tax savings on the 1031 exchange transaction and only had to pay taxes on the $40,000 shortfall.

What Are the Ownership or Title Requirements?

Another requirement of a 1031 exchange is that whoever sells the relinquished property has to be the same taxpayer that takes ownership of the new replacement property. The same person or entity who owned the old property has to be the same owner of the new property. If ABC Property, LLC, owned the property, then ABC Property, LLC, must be the buyer on title that purchased the replacement property in the 1031 exchange.

What about spouses? What if John was the sole owner of the relinquished property, but for loan purposes the bank required Lisa to take ownership of the replacement property? Can this be done? The answer would depend on whether the spouses were residents of a community property state or a separate property state. For a married couple who lives in a community property state, husband and wife are treated as if they each own 50 percent of the relinquished property under community property rules. In this scenario, if Lisa was on title to the replacement property, for tax purposes, both John and Lisa were deemed to own it together. This would be allowable for 1031 exchange purposes.

But what if the spouses lived in a separate property state? In that case, one is not deemed to own anything that is only titled under the other's name. Because Lisa did not own the relinquished property, she could not be the sole owner of the new replacement property for a valid 1031 exchange. For this couple, John would have to be on title to 100 percent of the replacement property for it to work for 1031 exchange purposes.

Typically, when an LLC sells a rental property it owns, the LLC must purchase the replacement property in order to have a valid 1031 exchange. There is an exception to this rule when it comes to single member LLCs, meaning that the LLC has only one owner or member. When this occurs, the LLC is basically disregarded or ignored for federal tax purposes. The LLC would not have to file its own federal tax return—instead, the income and expenses of the LLC would be ultimately reported on the LLC member's tax return. If the LLC owned a rental property and the LLC was 100 percent owned by John, he would report that rental property on his personal income tax return.

This is relevant for 1031 exchange purposes because since a single member LLC is disregarded or ignored for tax purposes, it's treated as if the LLC owner owns that property anyway. This means that if the LLC sold the property and John purchased the replacement property, it would still be a valid 1031 exchange because the LLC is a disregarded entity that is owned 100 percent by John. As tax advisors, we see this happen quite often because lenders usually are more comfortable lending to the individual than to the LLC itself. On the other hand, the investor may have personally owned the property being sold, but wants to use a new single member LLC to take title to the replacement property for asset protection reasons. Both situations are completely allowable under the 1031 exchange rules.

Another common question we get regarding the ownership or title requirements is whether someone can change title to the property right before or after the exchange. Let's say, for example, that Kevin did a 1031 exchange and purchased the replacement property in his personal name. Immediately after the closing on the transaction, Kevin decides to partner with another investor, Mike. Kevin and Mike form an LLC that will be treated as a partnership for tax purposes. Mike has $200,000 of cash that he is going to contribute into the partnership, and Kevin has his replacement property from his 1031 exchange that is worth $200,000. Kevin wants to contribute his replacement property into the new partnership.

If Kevin had decided to do that, it would likely have blown the 1031 exchange that he recently completed. The reason for this goes back to one of the first requirements we discussed about what qualifies for a replacement property: For a valid 1031 exchange, the property must be used in a trade or business or be held for investment. In a rental property context, you would look to whether the property was held for investment. And in Kevin's example, if the property was contributed to the partnership immediately after he purchased it in the exchange, it's likely that the IRS could argue that Kevin himself didn't own or hold that property for investment purposes. If the IRS is successful in arguing that upon an audit, Kevin's entire exchange could be disallowed, and he might have to pay all the taxes on the sale of his relinquished property.

In this situation, it would generally be best for Kevin to hold title to the replacement property in his personal name for at least one calendar year before contributing it to the partnership. The longer he could hold the property in his personal name, the higher his chances of success would be in the event of an IRS audit.

Which Taxpayers are Eligible for 1031 Exchange?

Virtually any taxpayer who wants to take advantage of deferring their taxes on the sale of a rental property is eligible to utilize a 1031 exchange, including:

- Individuals
- Single member LLCs
- Partnerships
- S corporations
- C corporations
- Trusts
- Charitable organizations
- Retirement accounts

1031 Exchange Intermediary

For a valid 1031 exchange, it is important to note that you need to hire an independent third party to act as your qualified 1031 exchange accommodator or intermediary. You cannot do the transaction on your own or be your own intermediary. You cannot sell your existing property first and then get a 1031 exchange intermediary involved after the sale closes, either—you must have an intermediary involved before you sell your relinquished property.

As you can already see, there are many time, money, and titling requirements for a 1031 exchange. Not meeting one or more of these can end up costing you a lot in taxes. As a result, we recommend that you work with a company that has extensive experience in acting as an intermediary and helping clients with 1031 exchanges. You should look for an intermediary company that is both insured and bonded for its intermediary work. You may also want to find a company that holds your exchange funds in "segregated accounts" as opposed to commingled accounts. With segregated accounts, your funds are held in their own account with the intermediary, which are separate from the intermediary's other clients' funds. *Commingled* is just what it sounds like—all your funds are in an account with the intermediary's other clients' funds. In our experience, that can be a recipe for disaster, so using an intermediary who has segregated client funds may be in your best interest.

Your 1031 exchange intermediary will have a few different roles and responsibilities in your exchange. They are going to help you with paperwork and any required documents for the exchange. They will hold on to your money for you, and they should act as one of your professional advisors during the process to answer your questions. They should also help you stay compliant with all the rules and time requirements to ensure you complete a valid exchange.

Who can be your intermediary? Remember, the person or entity serving as your intermediary needs to be an independent third party. But like a lot of things in the tax code, unfortunately, the IRS doesn't clearly or directly define who can be an intermediary. Instead, the IRS dictates who *cannot* be an intermediary. This list of "disqualified" people or entities includes the following:
- Yourself
- Anyone related to you (that is, a family member)
- An entity or business owned by a family member
- Anyone who works for you
- Anyone who works for one of these disqualified people or companies
- Anyone with a business or professional relationship with you (that is, your attorney, CPA, financial advisor, etc.)

If you and your tax advisor have determined that a 1031 exchange is a good strategy to help defer taxes on the sale of your investment properties, one of the first next steps is to find an intermediary to help you with the transaction.

Who Is It Ideal For?

A 1031 exchange is a great strategy to defer taxes when you sell an investment property—the larger the tax gain, the higher the potential tax benefit you might receive with a 1031 exchange. A 1031 exchange could be a good potential strategy if you have any of these situations:

- You are facing a tax bill for the potential sale of your property that you either don't want to pay right now or don't have the funds to pay right now.
- You do not have any other tax losses or benefits that could be used to offset the gain and reduce the taxes due.
- You are looking to reinvest your money from the sale of the property into additional investment properties.
- You want to get out of the current real estate market and reinvest in another market.
- You want to get out of the residential rental market and into the non-residential rental market.
- You want to trade up to larger or better-performing properties.
- You want to reduce the property management headache from owning multiple properties by replacing them with just one property.
- Your existing properties have been fully depreciated and you want some additional depreciation from new properties to reduce your taxes each year.

WHAT DOES IT ALL MEAN?

A 1031 exchange is an extremely powerful strategy to defer taxes on the sale of investment properties. When you sell the property and replace it with other replacement properties, the IRS allows you to defer the capital gains taxes into future years. It is also possible to sell one type of real estate and reinvest in other types of real estate, as long as the properties are investment properties.

To be eligible for a 1031 exchange, you must identify your replacement property within 45 days of selling your relinquished property, and you must also close on the replacement property within 180 days from the date of the sale. The transaction must be done through a 1031 exchange intermediary who helps to facilitate the transaction. To be eligible for the full tax-deferral benefit, the replacement property must equal or exceed the relinquished property's net sales price, as well as the net equity.

If all the rules are met, you receive the ability to defer all the taxes that you would otherwise pay to the IRS. In situations where some of the rules are not met, you may still have an opportunity to defer part of the taxes from the gain into future tax years.

There are many rules and pitfalls to be aware of when it comes to utilizing a 1031 exchange as a tax strategy. Proactively planning with your tax advisor can help ensure that you receive the maximum tax benefits and protect your money from the IRS.

CHAPTER 8
1031 EXCHANGES GONE WRONG

"The only real mistake is the one from which we learn nothing."

—HENRY FORD

Now that you know how powerful a 1031 exchange can be, it's important to also discuss what can happen when this strategy is not implemented correctly. In this chapter, we will be sharing two tax horror stories from 1031 exchange transactions; they will demonstrate what the tax impact could be when a 1031 exchange is not implemented correctly, and more important, what the tax cost could be in a bad situation.

STORY #1: Syndication Slipup

Although Jennifer's condo had been a good investment in terms of appreciation and cash flow, it had been difficult to manage. Between break-ins, floods, and roof leaks, Jennifer spent countless hours managing the property and its tenants. She finally listed the condo for sale and received a purchase offer.

After owning it for over ten years, she had taken quite a bit of depreciation on the property. Plus, with the recent appreciation, Jennifer was looking at a pretty sizable gain with an estimated tax bill of about

$50,000. She had plans to take her money and trade up into larger apartment deals, and she could get access to large properties with great cash flow and appreciation by investing in a syndication. A syndication is generally an LLC owned by numerous investors who pool their money together to invest in larger apartments or commercial properties. One benefit to the syndication investor is the ability to sit back and collect distributions while the sponsor takes care of the investment and manages the asset.

This was exactly what Jennifer was looking for. She was ready to trade up from her condo to a larger property, and she loved the idea that she could do so while removing herself from property management and not needing to deal with potential tenant issues.

Jennifer learned from her investor friend that a 1031 exchange could be used to help her defer the $50,000 in capital gains taxes that she was facing on the sale of her condo. The syndication deal was offering above-average returns, and many investors were jumping on board. In Jennifer's mind, this would be a simple transaction: Sell the condo and reinvest that money in the apartment syndication LLC. Because she already knew exactly where she would invest her money, Jennifer felt she did not need the help of a CPA or a 1031 exchange intermediary. After all, to her it seemed like a very easy transaction, didn't it? It wasn't until after she completed the sale of her condo that she realized she had made some big and costly mistakes.

There were three issues with Jennifer's planned 1031 exchange. The first was that her plan involved investing in a syndication's LLC interest instead of direct ownership in a property. As previously mentioned, membership interests of an LLC or a partnership are not an eligible asset for 1031 exchange purposes. Even though the LLC used its investors' funds to purchase an apartment building, LLC membership interests are not considered real estate property, and thus not eligible for 1031 exchange treatment.

The second requirement Jennifer didn't meet was the title/ownership requirement. Remember, the manner in which you hold title to the relinquished property has to be the same way you hold title to the replacement property. In her situation, she owned the condo in her personal name, but the supposed "replacement property"—the apartment building—was now owned by the syndication LLC.

The third issue for Jennifer was that she did not work with a 1031 exchange intermediary. Because Jennifer had thought this would be a pretty straightforward transaction, she simply closed on the sale of the condo herself. Her plan had been to take the cash and give it to the syndication LLC to purchase her ownership interest. As discussed in the last chapter, it is a requirement for a valid 1031 exchange to go through a qualified intermediary. This is true no matter how simple or straightforward the transaction may be. Unfortunately for Jennifer, because the condo was sold without the 1031 exchange intermediary, the entire transaction was automatically made taxable. Jennifer was not able to defer any of the capital gains taxes on the sale of her condo, and had to pay all of that to the IRS in the year the property was sold.

STORY #2: Shortfall Stumble

Robin and his wife, Mary, had owned their rental property in California for a few years. Although the property had appreciated quite a bit, it did not provide much cash flow on a month-to-month basis. Robin and Mary were getting close to retiring, and they wanted to move their investment to other geographical areas that would generate more monthly cash flow so that they would have additional disposable cash once they stopped working at their full-time jobs.

When the California market was at its peak, Robin and Mary decided it was their time to get out. Their plan was to sell their California rental and then use that money to buy four more rentals in Ohio. Based on their projections, the Ohio rentals could provide them with the cash flow they wanted. If they could sell their property for $915,000, the taxable gain on the transaction would have been $200,000. Between federal and state taxes, they were looking at a tax bill of close to $70,000. To avoid this tax, Robin and Mary's tax advisor recommended they consider a 1031 exchange.

For this transaction, Robin and Mary hired a 1031 exchange intermediary. Within days of being listed on the market, their California property sold for the full asking price of $915,000. After the couple paid off the mortgage of around $485,000, the net cash funds received by the 1031 exchange intermediary at closing was $430,000.

As they headed into retirement, Robin and Mary decided they would be more conservative when it came to investing. Instead of using leverage, they decided to purchase the four Ohio rentals using all cash. They used the $430,000 of funds from the sale of the California property, along with about $40,000 of additional cash, to acquire four replacement properties, within the 180-day replacement time period. The total purchase price for the four replacement properties was close to $470,000.

Robin and Mary thought they had done everything correctly. They had hired a qualified 1031 exchange intermediary, had used all the money that was available at closing to purchase the replacement properties, and had put an additional $40,000 into the new replacement properties. They were extremely shocked to find out that they had failed the 1031 exchange and would be required to pay the full taxes on this transaction. What had gone wrong?

In Robin and Mary's situation, they used all their 1031 exchange funds from the sale of their relinquished property and reinvested those funds into four replacement properties, so they met the equity replacement target amount. What they did not do was meet the purchase price replacement target. They sold their relinquished California property for $915,000, which meant they needed to acquire replacement properties with a total cost of $915,000 or more. In their situation, the total purchase price of the four replacement properties was only $470,000. Since the shortfall of $445,000 was larger than the $200,000 gain on the sale of the California property, the result was that Robin and Mary's entire transaction became taxable in that year. As a result, they had to pay close to $70,000 in capital gains taxes for that year. The 1031 exchange provided them with no tax benefits for this transaction.

Believe it or not, this is a common mistake that we often see with 1031 exchange transactions. In a 1031 exchange, the replacement property's purchase price should equal or exceed the relinquished property's sales price, not the net cash proceeds available at closing after loan payoff. This is an area of great confusion for many investors and can be a tax trap for the unwary.

What Else Can Go Wrong in a 1031 Exchange?

Because of the numerous requirements for a valid 1031 exchange, the list of "what can go wrong" in an exchange is, in fact, countless. It's like Murphy's Law: If you think it could go wrong, then it probably has gone wrong for someone at some point in time. Here are a few other aspects of a 1031 exchange that we've seen go awry.

Turning in your 45-day identification list late

As we discussed in the previous chapter, your list of potential replacement properties must be in writing. You can turn in your written identification list to your intermediary in person, via email, fax, or regular mail. But what if you show up at your intermediary's office and give it to them on the forty-sixth day? In this situation, you would have already failed the exchange. You may be wondering *But how is the IRS going to know that I missed this deadline?"* Well, it's going to know because you are required by law to disclose this date on the 1031 exchange Form 8824 that gets filed with your tax return. If audited, you and your intermediary are required to provide proof of the date your properties were identified in writing to your intermediary. If you did not meet the date requirements for a 1031 exchange but you still report the sale as a valid exchange on your tax return, that could be considered tax fraud. If you're ever audited and it's discovered by the IRS or a taxing agency, the result could be massive taxes and penalties. Why take that risk?

Paying too much for the replacement property

In a 1031 exchange, you are often up against the clock. Imagine the scenario where you are bearing down on your 180-day deadline for closing on your replacement property. Your internal stress is building. You have a property in mind, but you are currently in a bidding war with two other parties. You've offered $500,000 for the property, which you feel is a good price for this asset. But according to your agent, you've been outbid so far. You are ready and willing to increase your offer, and actually do increase it to $550,000. You tell yourself that you need to close soon; otherwise, you will fail your 1031 exchange. This means you'll have to pay a boatload of taxes for the sale of your relinquished property. Congratulations, the seller accepts your new offer of $550,000 and you've won the bidding war!

But what just happened? Based on your previous research, you believed $500,000 was a fair price for this asset. But you just ended up paying 10 percent more than what you thought the property was worth! Most seasoned investors would probably agree that that's not a good start for an investment property. Before jumping the gun to increase your purchase price, consider meeting with your tax advisor once again to determine how much in taxes you are projected to save by doing a 1031 exchange. That way, you can compare the tax cost against the added cost of the property and make an informed investment decision on whether to walk away or continue to pursue this deal.

Buying a bad asset

Along the same lines, instead of paying too much for a property, what if you just make a bad purchase altogether? Imagine that same 180-day clock is ticking down for you. You sold your relinquished property, previously identified five potential replacement properties, and successfully closed on two of them—but you need to buy one more property to satisfy your exchange requirements. Two of the remaining three properties on your identification list fell through for various reasons.

There's one property left on your identification list. Based on some additional due diligence you've done recently, you've discovered a few issues on this property that concern you. The actual rents that you will be receiving from your tenants don't match what the seller had originally advertised to you. In addition, there was a lot more deferred maintenance on the property that could end up being very costly. The seller has found out that you are doing a 1031 exchange and are up against the clock, so he is not willing to renegotiate the price. What do you do?

Unfortunately, we've seen many situations like this in which investors justify a bad purchase simply because they didn't want to pay taxes on their capital gains, so they let the tax tail wag the investment dog.

In almost all of these situations, our clients have regretted purchasing this last property because it turned out to be a bad investment. Make sure you evaluate and consider everything as a whole, and don't rush into any investment purchases just because you are deferring taxes using a 1031 exchange.

Not having an intermediary

One of the mistakes that we saw with Jennifer's story was not getting an intermediary involved prior to the sale of her property. Unfortunately, this is a common and costly error that we see time and time again. The time to get an intermediary involved is prior to the sale of your investment properties. If you have already closed on the sale of your "relinquished" property, it is too late to do a 1031 exchange. Remember, you cannot be your own intermediary. Your qualified intermediary is going to help you prepare your exchange documents and help you with your closings. It is always best to get your intermediary involved as early as possible—even before you list the property for sale!

Receiving a check at the close of escrow

What if you have just closed on the sale of your "relinquished" property, and your escrow company has given you a check for the net proceeds? Yes, you guessed it; this would violate the 1031 exchange rules as well. Usually this happens in situations where the seller is either not familiar with 1031 exchange rules or has not yet hired a qualified intermediary.

What is the problem with receiving a check at the close of escrow? Remember, one of the rules is that you cannot touch the money. Even if you do not cash the check and instead put that money directly into the replacement property that you will purchase, this is still a violation of the 1031 exchange rules. In the eyes of the IRS, even though you didn't cash the check, you received it and you had control of the money. The point is that you *could* have cashed the check. For 1031 exchange purposes, having the check in your possession means you have the money.

Not communicating with your advisors

As you can see from the various stories in this chapter, not communicating proactively with your tax advisors can cost you a lot of money in taxes when a 1031 exchange rule is not met. The best time to plan proactively for your transaction is before the sale of your property. The first step is to work with your tax advisor to determine what the taxes would be if you do not do a 1031 exchange. If there are little to no taxes on the sale of a property, then there may be no reason to even do a 1031 exchange.

Once you determine that a 1031 exchange will help reduce your taxes, the next step is to interview an exchange intermediary and get them to be part of your team. With everyone on the same page, your odds of making a mistake can be diminished drastically. Remember that your advisors cannot help you or protect you from land mines if they don't know what you are doing. Don't be afraid to reach out to your advisors. That's what they are there for. A quick email can go a long way to keep you from stepping on the proverbial 1031 exchange land mines.

Ownership limitations with a tenant in a common 1031 exchange

This is a common mistake for investors involved in 1031 exchange transactions involving a tenant in common ownerships. For example, Karl and Betty own a property in their personal name but want to sell it in a 1031 exchange to move into a better asset or a better market. They have found a potential replacement property, but due to the purchase price or the financing needed for the deal, they can't afford to purchase the entire property on their own. They decide to purchase the property as a Tenant in Common (TIC) owner with their friend Karen. Based on the agreement, Karl and Betty will own 40 percent of the property, and Karen will own 60 percent of the property. For tax purposes, if someone owns 40 percent of the property as a TIC, then 40 percent of the purchase price of the property needs to be paid by the 40 percent TIC owner. Yes, that's right—exactly 40 percent.

Where do people get in trouble with 1031 exchanges in these situations? Let's assume that for Karl and Betty, they need to purchase a property for $100,000 in order to meet the purchase price requirement for their 1031 exchange. If the replacement property they are investing in with Karen has a total purchase price of $190,000, their share of the purchase price at 40 percent would only be $76,000. In this situation, the TIC purchase agreement only requires them to put in $76,000, so they would have had a $24,000 shortfall.

What if they were to contribute more than their required share of $76,000? Since Karl and Betty knew they needed to contribute $100,000 in order to defer all of their taxes, maybe they'll decide they might as well put all that money into the TIC, even though their agreement only required $76,000. Believe it or not, this could still be a problem for Karl and Betty. Remember, the TIC purchase agreement requires them to put in only $76,000 for their 40 percent ownership. If they contribute more than that, they need to revise their ownership percentage accordingly in order to have a valid 1031 exchange. Otherwise, they will still have to recognize $24,000 as taxable gain for the 1031 exchange shortfall, even though they had actually contributed more than what was required.

When Is a 1031 Exchange Not an Ideal Choice?

The tax benefits of a 1031 exchange sound amazing on paper and can be amazing in real life too. If you think about it, why let Uncle Sam slow down your investing plans if you don't have to? There's no limit to the number of 1031 exchanges you can do in your lifetime. As morbid as it may sound, if you want to be a lifelong real estate investor, there's nothing stopping you from doing 1031 exchanges until you pass away. In the tax world, this is commonly referred to as the "swap until you drop" strategy.

But before you jump on the bandwagon to do a 1031 exchange for every property you want to sell, let's look at some situations where doing a 1031 exchange may not be an ideal choice.

Selling a property for a loss

The benefit of doing a 1031 exchange is the ability to postpone paying taxes that might be due if you sold your property for a gain. If you sell your property at a loss, then you should not have any taxes to pay on the sale anyway. In that scenario, there is no reason to do a 1031 exchange. You should also be able to deduct the loss on your tax return in the year you sell your property. Since selling your investment property for a loss can actually reduce your taxes in most situations, a 1031 exchange would not be appropriate.

Cost versus benefit

A 1031 exchange may not make sense when your costs outweigh the benefits. This may happen if you are selling your property where the taxes due on the sale may be small. In that situation, you should make sure that the fees you would pay to your intermediary, your CPA, and any other advisors to assist you with the transaction don't exceed the savings from the tax deferral. If the taxes to be owed on the sale are relatively small, you should make sure that the potential stress of doing a 1031 exchange is worth it. Ask yourself: *Are the tax savings worth the hassle?*

Allowable losses to offset the gain

Perhaps you will have a net loss in the current year from your rental properties or from other passive investments, or perhaps you had generated these similar losses—from rental properties in a previous year—that haven't been utilized yet. Generally these net passive losses can be used to offset taxes on the gain from the sale of an investment property.

A similar strategy can be applied to capital losses. Gain on sale of rental properties is treated as capital gains income on your tax return, and capital losses can be used to offset capital gains income on your tax return. So perhaps you have stocks in your portfolio that have decreased in value since you purchased them. Or maybe you sold some stock at a loss in a previous year and you still have some leftover capital losses carrying forward to be used in the current year. In either of these scenarios, you should evaluate how much of the taxes on the sale of your rental would be after utilizing the offsets by your capital losses. If the resulting net tax to be owed is small, then it may not be worth it to do a 1031 exchange.

Another item that can reduce your tax gain on the sale of your investment property can be any net operating losses that you may have. Outside of just your rental property or other passive investments, maybe you have an overall net operating loss carryforward from a previous tax year that hasn't been utilized yet. We typically see net operating losses occur when a taxpayer generates negative taxable income. If you are expecting a gain on the sale of an investment property in the current tax year and you have a remaining net operating loss in the current or prior year, then doing a 1031 exchange may not be necessary to save in taxes.

Getting out of real estate

If you are not interested in reinvesting your funds into more real estate, a 1031 exchange may not work for you. As you've seen with an exchange, you are selling existing real estate and replacing it with more real estate. Tax-deferral savings aside, is it your plan to invest in more real estate? Maybe you've been investing in real estate for a while but now have an opportunity to generate better returns outside of real estate. Or maybe you've been successful and done well with your real estate investing, and you are just interested in diversifying into other asset classes such as stocks, notes, or start-up companies. Whatever the reason is, if you don't want to be tied to more real estate, then doing a 1031 exchange is not a good choice in your situation.

Partial reinvestment

Maybe you do want to invest in more real estate, but you just don't want to have to reinvest all the net proceeds from selling your relinquished properties. For example, let's say you sold a rental property and are now looking at a 1031 exchange. The equity replacement target is $400,000 in order to receive the full tax-deferral benefit. You are interested in reinvesting some money into real estate again but do not want to reinvest the entire $400,000. Maybe you decided that you only want to reinvest $250,000 back into more real estate and plan to keep the remaining $150,000 of cash for other non–real estate investments.

Using a 1031 exchange in this scenario means that the $150,000 of proceeds you kept would be considered income. Although you only reinvested part of the proceeds back into real estate, you can still do a 1031 exchange and receive partial tax deferral. If you are contemplating a partial reinvestment of your 1031 exchange funds, make sure to run the numbers beforehand with your tax advisor to ensure that you will still receive tax-deferral benefits that exceed your costs of doing the exchange.

Getting out of a partnership

As you will recall, one requirement of the 1031 exchange is based on title and ownership. The taxpayer who owns the relinquished property has to be the same taxpayer who acquires the replacement properties. If you are one of four partners in an LLC that owns an investment property, the replacement property generally needs to be purchased by the LLC in order to meet the 1031 exchange title rules. This means that you would still have to buy with your partners, even if you don't want to be in business with them any longer. You are generally not allowed to have the LLC sell the property and then purchase the replacement property personally because the seller (the LLC) and the buyer (you) are different taxpayers.

Fortunately, there is a strategy to get around this; it's commonly referred to as a "drop and swap."

How to "Drop and Swap" for a 1030 Exchange

Chris was a partner in an LLC with his two brothers. The LLC has owned a shopping center for more than twenty years that was worth $6,000,000, and its adjusted tax basis was $1,400,000. If the LLC sold the property outright, the LLC's three partners would each have to pay taxes on a third of the $4,600,000 of gain. Chris and his brothers were interested in a 1031 exchange, but they all wanted to go their separate ways regarding future investments. In order to accomplish this, we helped them implement the drop and swap strategy, which involves multiple steps:

Step 1: Re-title the property—Title of the property ownership was changed from the LLC as 100 percent owner to each brother owning one-third of the property as tenants in common.

Step 2: Update the operations of the property—Chris and his brothers changed the rental agreements, property management agreement, and other contracts to reflect the property's new owners. They notified their property manager and other vendors that the property was now owned by the three of them as TICs (tenants in common). Going forward, the property manager would collect all rent checks, pay all property expenses, and then deposit a third of the net income every month into each owner's personal bank account, based on their respective ownership percent.

Step 3: Hold the property as an investment property—Chris and his brothers would continue to hold and rent out the property as TIC owners. In order to help substantiate that the property was held "for investment" purposes by each of the brothers as TIC owners, we recommended that they continue to own and rent out the property for at least three tax years.

Step 4: Dissolve the LLC—The next step was to legally dissolve the LLC and file final tax returns for the LLC within 2½ months after the LLC's dissolution date. Once the LLC transferred title of the property to the three brothers, it wound up its operations. After all lingering expenses were paid for and remaining money transferred out, the brothers could dissolve the LLC with the Secretary of State, then file a short-year final tax return for the LLC within 2½ months after the dissolution date.

For 1031 exchange purposes, the LLC couldn't sell the property and have each brother purchase his own replacement properties in his own name. The issue would then have been that the IRS could disallow the transaction by pointing out that as individuals, they did not hold the property as an "investment" because the holding period had been so short. Therefore, in order to defer paying taxes on the eventual gain on sale, they implemented the drop and swap. They "dropped" the property out of the LLC into the hands of each brother by changing title. Then the brothers rented out the property for the recommended three tax years.

Keep in mind that these "tax years" don't necessarily need to be three whole calendar years. This can be met in as little as fourteen months if those fourteen months straddle three tax years (for example, December Year 1 to January Year 3). Based on 1031 exchange case law, three tax return years is the recommended time frame to substantiate that the property was held for investment purposes. Once they reached Year 3, they sold the property and each brother did his own 1031 exchange and "swapped" into his own replacement properties. The swap and drop strategy allowed them to sell the property, use 1031 exchange to defer the taxes, and also to go their own separate ways for future investments.

As you can see, utilizing what is referred to as the drop and swap strategy takes a significant amount of planning and time, as there are a lot of nuances and action items that must take place. This is definitely a strategy that you want to work with your tax advisor on well in advance of actually selling the property.

WHAT DOES IT ALL MEAN?

Even the most well-intentioned taxpayers can make a tax mistake, and a 1031 exchange transaction has a lot of rules, deadlines, and hidden traps. Missing the 45-day identification or not getting an intermediary involved at the sale of the property can immediately destroy your ability to defer taxes using a 1031 exchange. On the other hand, not meeting the purchase price or equity target of your replacement property can create some taxes while still allowing you to defer a portion of your taxes.

As with most things in the tax world, the 1031 exchange is not a one-size-fits-all strategy. It can be a great deferral strategy if you are facing a large tax bill and are looking to reinvest that money into more investment properties. Alternatively, a 1031 exchange may not be a good fit if you have little to no taxes due or if you simply want to get out of real estate as an investment vehicle.

Within the complicated tax rules of the 1031 exchange, there are also small loopholes that can help you circumvent some of the limitations of this technique. Planning ahead and getting your tax advisor involved before selling your investment property can help you protect your tax savings and continue to grow your real estate portfolio.

CHAPTER 9

CASHING OUT OF A 1031 EXCHANGE WITHOUT PAYING TAXES

"You can have your cake and eat it too."

—**BOB DYLAN**

A 1031 exchange is a great tax strategy to help an investor sell a property for a gain and reinvest that money into additional properties—all without paying any taxes to the IRS at that time. In a 1031 exchange, the higher the appreciation, the bigger the tax savings.

One of the main rules to a 1031 exchange is that no cash is taken out of the transaction. Let's say you are selling a rental property and looking at a $50,000 gain, but instead of reinvesting all the required money into your replacement property, you decided to take out $20,000 of cash for personal use. In this scenario, you would pay taxes on the $20,000 because that cash is considered "boot" and becomes taxable immediately. However, you still get to defer taxes on the remaining $30,000 of gain from the transaction.

One question we get is whether it is possible to take cash out of a 1031 exchange transaction without paying any taxes at that time. That can absolutely be done. However, as usual with most things in the tax world, there are the right ways and the wrong ways to access cash with this vehicle.

Refinancing the Property to Take Cash Out

One of the most common ways to access cash from an investment property is with refinances.

Todd recently completed a 1031 exchange. In the exchange, he had a rental property with $200,000 of equity that he sold for $500,000. Todd purchased a duplex for $650,000 as his replacement property and contributed the entire $200,000 of equity from his old property into it. After completing the 1031 exchange, Todd decided he wanted to invest in more properties—he found another rental that could provide great cash flow, but he did not have any cash on hand to invest.

Todd had $200,000 of equity in the new duplex that he wanted to access, so he went to the bank to refinance the duplex to pull out $200,000 of cash. Although Todd received cash by refinancing his replacement property, that cash was not considered boot and was therefore tax-free loan proceeds, so it could still be tax-deferred.

Todd's plan was to use the refinance proceeds to purchase more rental properties. But what if Todd did not end up doing that? What if Todd was not able to find any good properties, and he decided to take the loan proceeds to start a business, invest in some stocks, or just buy himself a nice new home? In these scenarios, Todd could still receive the refinance proceeds without violating the 1031 exchange transaction. There are no restrictions on how the loan proceeds from the refinance are utilized.

In addition, there are no restrictions as to how much cash is taken out in a refinance. If Todd's duplex appreciated significantly immediately after his purchase and the bank was willing to let him take a cash-out refinance of $300,000, Todd could access all that money tax-free, without violating the 1031 exchange transaction.

You may be wondering: *How long do you need to wait after the exchange closes before you can refinance?* Is it a week, a month, a year? It can be sooner than you may think.

As soon as you close on the replacement property, you can work with a lender to start on the refinancing of that property to start pulling your cash out. The refinance cash out does not at all violate the 1031 exchange transaction that you just implemented. The entire gain on the sale of the rental property continues to be tax-deferred, provided that there is a business purpose to the refinancing.

What if you wanted to do a cash-out refinance before entering into a 1031 exchange transaction? Would you receive the same tax benefits? Unfortunately, that would be a lot trickier. Whether the refinance of a property before the 1031 exchange transaction resulted in taxable boot really could come down to the timing of the refinance.

There's no hard and fast rule written in the IRS code as to when you can refinance a property before a 1031 exchange. But based on case law and other previous IRS rulings, it's generally recommended that any cash-out refinances are done at least six months to a year before the sale of your property. If you do that, you are generally in the safe zone. A lot can happen in six to twelve months, so it could be hard for the IRS to argue that you were refinancing the property for the sole purpose of taking cash out of the future 1031 exchange.

What if you refinanced the relinquished property a week or two before the property was sold? In that situation, it's very likely that the IRS would assess taxes on the money taken out in the refinance as taxable boot. Taking out your loan application after you have signed the agreement to sell your property is often a dead giveaway that you were trying to take cash out of the eventual exchange—and that would not be a good fact pattern for an investor trying to defer taxes.

Primary Home and 1031 Exchange Combination

One of the underlying principles for a 1031 exchange is that the property must be an investment property. So selling or purchasing a primary residence doesn't qualify for 1031 exchange purposes. This means that if you sell an investment property, you cannot buy a primary home as your replacement property. And if you sell your primary home, you cannot use a 1031 exchange to buy an investment property.

There are, of course, exceptions to this rule. If the property used to be your primary residence, and you later moved out and then converted it to a rental property, it could be eligible for a 1031 exchange. As long as you can show that the property was held for investment purposes at the time of the sale, it should qualify for 1031 exchange tax benefits. A common question we get is "How long does it need to be a rental in order to qualify for 1031 exchange treatment?" Once again, there is no tax world hard-line rule as to the number of days the property must be a rental to prove that it was an investment property. It could be as short as a month, but if that's the case, you better have a compelling fact pattern showing why you rented it out and then all of a sudden you are selling it.

Let's assume you move out of your primary home and do turn it into a rental. The tenant signs a one-year lease contract and everything is going well. However, thirty days later, you receive an unsolicited offer from someone to buy the property with the tenant in place, and they make an offer you can't refuse. That property may still be eligible for 1031 exchange purposes because you can show that you intended it to be a long-term rental property, which the signed one-year lease and unsolicited offer both can help support.

Alternatively, if you simply move out of your home, rent it out on Airbnb for a few weeks, and simultaneously list it for sale on the Multiple Listing Service (MLS), odds are that a 1031 exchange won't be allowed because it's difficult to prove that your intent was to keep the property long-term as a rental property. Generally speaking, if you move out of your primary residence and then rent it out, it's probably best to rent it for at least twelve months if you plan to sell it in a 1031 exchange. If you can't get to twelve months, a rental period straddling two tax return years would probably be your next best option.

In a 1031 exchange, if you sell a rental property that used to be your primary residence, there may be a way to get cash out of the sale transaction at closing. For primary homes, the IRS allows taxpayers to exclude up to $250,000 of gain from their tax returns if they are single or $500,000 for a married couple. This tax benefit is available for a property that you live in as your primary home for at least two of the previous five years. This benefit can be combined with a 1031 exchange tax deferral for primary homes that are later turned into rentals. This means that you can exclude the first $250,000/$500,000 of gain from taxes, and also defer any additional gains using a 1031 exchange.

Let's go over an example of how this could work. For simplicity's sake, we will assume no depreciation and no selling costs in the following story.

Andre lived in a condo in Huntington Beach that was one block away from the ocean. He originally purchased it in 2010 for $450,000 and lived there as his primary home. In December 2014, Andre moved out of his home and turned it into a rental, and a few years later, he sold the property for $750,000 on November 1, 2017.

At the time of the sale, the outstanding mortgage on the property was $350,000, so Andre had a total gain of $300,000 from the sale. Based on the dates, Andre met the two years of the five-year rule for the home sale exclusion. That meant he could receive up to $250,000 of gain completely tax-free. After that, there would be $50,000 of taxable gains remaining from this transaction.

Sales price: $750,000

Cost basis: −$450,000

Total gain: $300,000

Primary home exclusion: −$250,000

Remaining taxable gain: $50,000

Because Andre qualified for the primary home exclusion, he would be able to take out $250,000 of cash from the transaction completely free from taxes. Since Andre was intending to reinvest in more rental properties, he could use a 1031 exchange to defer the taxes on the remaining $50,000. After factoring in the primary home sale exclusion, Andre could defer taxes on the remaining $50,000 as long as he met the new lowered purchase price and equity target amounts below using a 1031 exchange.

$750,000	Sales Price	$750,000	Sales Price
($250,000)	Primary Home Exclusion	($350,000)	Outstanding Mortgage
$500,000	New Purchase Price Target	$400,000	Equity Replacement Target
		($250,000)	Primary Home Exclusion
		$150,000	New Equity Replacement Target

Effectively, the primary home sale exclusion and the 1031 exchange could have been utilized together to allow Andre to take tax-free cash out of his 1031 exchange and also defer taxes on any remaining gains. The result would be that there would be no taxes due at that time on any of the gains from the sale of the condo.

There are a few things to watch out for using these combined strategies. First, it is important to note that this only works if the property is a rental at the time of the sale. If the condo was first a rental and Andre turned it into his primary home by moving into it, then a 1031 exchange would not be allowed if Andre was using the condo as his primary home at the time of the property sale. And this strategy does not work as well if the property becomes a primary residence again after it had become a rental. For example, imagine the life of a property using this time frame:

Primary $\longrightarrow$ *Rental* $\longrightarrow$ *Primary* $\longrightarrow$ *Rental*

First it was a primary residence. Then it became a rental. Then Andre moved back in. Finally, Andre moved out, and it became a rental one more time. If Andre had had this situation and then sold the property, he would not have been able to take advantage of the maximum $250,000 primary home sale exclusion. This is just another quirky thing in the tax code. In this situation, Andre would need to look at the total ownership period of the property. He would have to determine what percentage of time it was a primary residence versus the percentage of time it was a rental property. If we assume it was used 50 percent of the time as a primary residence and 50 percent of the time as a rental property, the maximum primary home gain exclusion available to Andre would have been $125,000 ($250,000 maximum × 50 percent).

The key takeaways here are that if you convert a primary residence into a rental property, we would not recommend moving back into it for tax purposes. You should also consider whether selling the property within three years of moving out can make sense in your situation from a tax and financial perspective.

Using Offset Strategies to Take Out Cash

As you may recall from the previous chapter, there are a few scenarios where having unused loss carryforwards could be utilized in lieu of a 1031 exchange. If you were expecting a tax gain on the sale of an investment property, then capital losses, passive activity losses, or net operating losses can carry forward from a previous tax year to help offset the tax gain.

In that same context, if you wanted to take cash out of a 1031 exchange transaction, the taxable boot from that cash could be offset with any of these loss carryforwards as well.

For example, let's piggyback off of Andre's previous example, but let's assume that the property was never a primary residence and thus didn't qualify for the Section 121 exclusion. But let's also assume Andre still wanted to take out $250,000 of cash from the sale of the property. How could he do this? If Andre had some stocks that decreased in value compared to his purchase price, he could sell those stocks to generate capital losses. Those capital losses could be deducted against the $250,000 of capital gain from Andre's cash taken out of the 1031 exchange transaction. If Andre had rental losses from his other properties in the current year or unused rental losses from previous years, those losses could also be utilized.

We often meet investors who tell us they decided not to do a 1031 exchange simply because they wanted to access part of their cash when they sold a property. But contrary to popular belief, it is possible to take cash out of a 1031 exchange transaction. Using the strategies discussed in this chapter, you can even have your cake and eat it too by cashing out and still avoiding the taxes! Just make sure to plan ahead accordingly so you do not fall victim to some of the traps for the unwary.

What's the End Game?

Over the years, we have met with investors who were not keen on the idea of 1031 exchanges for real estate. One of the biggest reasons people may shy away from a 1031 exchange is that this is simply a tax-deferral strategy and not a tax-elimination strategy. This means that, instead of paying taxes today when we sell our appreciated property, we are delaying, and instead will pay taxes in a future year. The good news, as we mentioned before, is that there are no limits to the number of 1031 exchanges you can do throughout your lifetime, but you are only deferring your taxes until the day you do *not* use a 1031 exchange.

However, many investors may not know that in addition to tax-deferral benefits, a 1031 exchange can also create permanent tax savings. If you want to, you can continue to use 1031 exchange transactions to receive permanently tax-free benefits with the swap until you drop method. At the date of your death, the IRS allows for a basis step-up. This means that your tax basis is no longer your original purchase price minus depreciation you have already taken—instead, your tax basis is now "stepped-up" to the fair market value of the investment properties at the date of death. As a result of step-up basis, if your beneficiaries decide to sell the properties they just inherited, they could pay *no* taxes on all of the appreciation of the properties that happened during your lifetime.

Take Ashley, for example. She bought her first single family rental, and a few years later, she sold that single-family rental to purchase a duplex in a 1031 exchange. Six years later, she sold the duplex and purchased an apartment building. Ashley held onto the apartment building for many years, and when she passed away, that apartment building was worth $2,820,000.

What is her tax basis in the properties? First, the amount needed to meet the target purchase price requirement does not result in additional tax basis; that portion of the replacement property purchase was tax-deferred as part of the 1031 exchange. However, to the extent that the purchase price of Ashley's replacement property exceeded the purchase price target, Ashley received additional tax basis for those excess amounts. This is commonly referred to in the tax world as "up-leg"—it reduces future taxable gain when an investor sells the property.

Ashley bought her first property for $120,000. She sold it for $400,000 and purchased the duplex for $500,000. The $100,000 difference between the purchase price of the duplex and the sales price of the single-family home gave her additional tax basis. So her tax basis rolling into the duplex should have been $220,000 ($120,000 original + $100,000 additional up-leg basis).

$500,000	Duplex Purchase Price
($400,000)	Single Family Sales Price (i.e. Replacement Property Target Purchase Price)
$100,000	Additional Tax Basis
$120,000	Single Family Purchase Price
$100,000	Additional Up-Leg
$220,000	Total Tax Basis in Duplex

A few years later, Ashley sold the duplex for $800,000 and purchased the apartment building for $1,400,000. Her increase in basis—attributable to the additional money spent on the apartment building—was $600,000 ($1,400,000 – $800,000). Her carryover tax basis going into the apartment building was $820,000 ($220,000 carryover basis from the duplex plus $600,000 additional up-leg basis):

$1,400,000	Apartment Purchase Price
($800,000)	Duplex Sales Price
$600,000	Additional Tax Basis
$220,000	Total Tax Basis in Duplex
$600,000	Additional Up-Leg
$820,000	Total Tax Basis in Apartment

Ashley lived many happy years as an investor owning that apartment building. The market did well, and the property was worth $2,820,000 in the year that Ashley passed away. If she had sold the property in a taxable transaction before she died, Ashley would have been sitting on $2,000,000 of gain on sale ($2,820,000 sale price minus $820,000 carryover tax basis). Assuming combined federal and state tax rates of 35 percent, Ashley would have been looking at a tax bill of at least $700,000 of the $2,000,000 of gain. But if she instead had held on to the property until she passed away and it was inherited by her kids, what would be the tax consequences to her kids?

Once an asset is inherited after the taxpayer's death, the beneficiary receives a full step-up in basis to the asset's fair market value. This means that upon inheriting the asset, her kids' tax basis in the apartment building would be the fair market value of $2,820,000 (the value of the property at Ashley's date of death). If Ashley's kids were to sell the apartment even one day after inheriting it for $2,820,000, then their gain on sale of the property would have been $0! That's because the sales price of the property is equal to their inherited basis at the fair market value.

In this example, Ashley has swapped until she dropped and passed along the property to her heirs, so her kids effectively ended up with tax-free gain on the property and all the previous properties that Ashley had done a 1031 exchange with during her lifetime. That's a huge tax benefit to Ashley's family. This one strategy could result in generation-altering investing!

WHAT DOES IT ALL MEAN?

A 1031 exchange can help defer a significant amount of taxes. Although there are many strict rules to the 1031 exchange, it may still be a viable tax strategy, even if you want to take cash out of the deal. After the close of a 1031 exchange transaction, it is possible to pull cash out of the replacement property and still have that money be tax-deferred. If you plan to pull cash out of the property before the property is sold in a 1031 exchange, the recommended waiting period is typically longer than six to twelve months.

In addition, if your property was a primary home that you turned into a rental property, it might be possible to pull cash out of the deal tax-free when you combine the primary home sale exclusion along with a 1031 exchange. If pulling cash out of a 1031 exchange in a taxable scenario, certain tax losses can be utilized to offset the taxes on this boot.

When implemented incorrectly, a 1031 exchange can result in costly mistakes. However, when implemented correctly, a 1031 exchange can be a wonderful tool that can create generational tax-free wealth from your real estate assets.

CHAPTER 10

SUPERCHARGING YOUR RETIREMENT WITH REAL ESTATE ASSETS

"Risk comes from not knowing what you're doing."

—WARREN BUFFETT

One of the easiest ways to reduce taxes is to put money into retirement accounts. After all, if you have the option of paying toward your own retirement versus paying the IRS, why would anyone choose to pay the IRS? One of the reasons many people choose not to fund their retirement accounts is that they would rather take that money and use it for real estate investments. For a lot of people, the decision comes down to whether they prefer:

    1. to pay some taxes and use the leftover money to invest in real estate

or

    2. to put the money into a retirement account to receive the tax benefits, but that money is locked up in the stock market

However, you are actually able to receive the tax benefits of putting money into a retirement account and *also* using that money in real estate. Contrary to popular belief, it does not mean you need to liquidate your retirement account and pay taxes and penalties. All you need to do is use self-directed investing to move your money from the stock market into real estate deals.

Jim had a Roth IRA (Individual Retirement Account) to which he had contributed over the years. Little by little, it grew to $100,000. Based on the advice of his financial planner, Jim invested his Roth IRA money in stocks, bonds, and advanced mutual funds, which had performed well over the years but Jim was never entirely comfortable with this. He had been a real estate investor his whole life, and he loved that his rental properties were tangible assets that he could see, touch, and visit. He was in control of his real estate investments and could buy, sell, or refinance when he felt the time was right. On the other hand, with the stock investments in his Roth IRA, Jim felt helpless. The value of his Roth IRA investments could go up or down on any given day, and there was nothing he could do to impact those fluctuations.

When we first started working with Jim a few years ago, he was excited to learn for the first time that he could use his Roth IRA to invest in real estate. Because money in the Roth IRA grows tax-free forever, Jim wanted to invest in cash-flowing and appreciating real estate assets, completely tax-free.

Jim's first step was to open a self-directed Roth IRA, so he interviewed self-directed IRA custodians and found a good fit. Part of the paperwork he filled out gave his new custodian the ability to request money from his current Roth IRA custodian, enabling a tax-free rollover of his Roth IRA in the stock market to the new self-directed Roth IRA. Then Jim started shopping for assets, and it wasn't long before he found a small single-family home for $80,000. This would allow him to use $80,000 of his Roth IRA funds to purchase the property and still keep $20,000 on hand in case of any unforeseen expenses that might come up for the rental. Jim's Roth IRA purchased the rental property, and title of the property was held in the Roth IRA.

Jim's Roth IRA rented out the property over the next five years with very few problems and was able to generate positive cash flow of $6,000 per year. All rental income was paid into the Roth IRA, and all rental expenses were paid out of the Roth IRA account.

Near the end of Year 5, the city approved a brand-new community center just down the street from where Jim's rental was located, and the value of that home skyrocketed overnight. Before long, developers were knocking on his door offering to purchase the property for more than $300,000—a dream come true for Jim! He quickly sold, and all of that money went back into his Roth IRA.

Since this transaction took place in his Roth IRA, Jim didn't have to pay taxes on any of his rental income over the years, plus the entire $300,000 from the sale of the property was also completely tax-free. In just a few years, Jim was able to turn his Roth IRA money from $100,000 to over $330,000, simply by moving it from the stock market into a great real estate deal.

As you can see, it's possible to control your retirement assets rather than to simply have that money sit passively in the stock market. In self-directed investing, the retirement account purchases and owns the investment property. Each month, rental income will be deposited into the retirement account and expenses are paid out of the retirement account. The net profit grows tax-advantaged within the retirement account each year. Eventually, when the investment is sold, the proceeds are deposited back into the retirement account and can be reinvested to continue the tax-advantaged growth.

If this is your first time learning about this strategy, don't worry. You are in good company with millions of Americans across the nation, because the vast majority of taxpayers are not familiar with the concept of self-directed investing. Many people have no idea that their retirement account can be used to invest directly in real estate rather than stocks, bonds, and mutual funds. In fact, the vast majority of tax *advisors* are not aware of this benefit that the IRS allows.

Self-directed investing is not a highly publicized strategy. Most stock brokers and financial advisors may not want people to know about this benefit, either because they are not comfortable with real estate investing or because they are not incentivized monetarily by the option of real estate investing. Think about it: If your financial advisor makes money only when you put your money in the stock market, why would they recommend you put your money in real estate instead?

At the end of the day, retirement money is one of your most precious buckets of money—it grows tax-advantaged year after year. Now that you know the benefits of this investing strategy, let's dive into the details to make sure we are using it correctly.

Regular Retirement Account Versus Self-Directed Retirement Account

So, what is the difference between a regular retirement account and a self-directed retirement account? The short answer is: not much. The only difference is what your retirement account is investing in.

A regular retirement account is usually opened with a financial institution or a bank. Once your account is open, you are provided a list of available stocks or mutual funds to choose from. For self-directed retirement accounts, you open up your account with a self-directed custodian who generally specializes in working with self-directed investors. After opening your account, you will tell the custodian what you want to invest your money in—the custodian will not give you a list to choose from.

Your investment decision is completely up to you. If you want, you can invest that money in a rental property on Main Street. Or if you prefer, you can use your retirement money to invest in a private note. You can even invest that money in your cousin's start-up business. Essentially, the self-directed custodian does not limit your investment to any particular asset or stocks.

That really is the only difference between a regular retirement account and a self-directed retirement account. How they operate, how much you can contribute, when you can take distributions, and the tax benefits of each retirement account are the same, whether it is a regular retirement account or a self-directed one.

To determine whether self-directed investing is right for you, here are two questions to ask yourself:

- What would I like to invest in, and where do I think I can get the best return?
- Do I want to keep my money in the stock market or do I want to invest in an asset with which I have more knowledge and control?

If you feel that you can do better with your retirement money in real estate than with the stock market, then self-directed investing may be a good strategy for you. It is important to note that although self-directed investing can be used for real estate, there are many other asset options, which we will go over later in this chapter.

Who Can Have a Self-Directed Account?

Almost anyone can have a self-directed retirement account. If you are eligible to have a regular IRA or Roth IRA, then you are eligible to have a self-directed IRA or Roth IRA. If you are eligible to open a SEP-IRA or Solo 401(k) for your business, then you can open a self-directed SEP-IRA or self-directed Solo 401(k). A SEP-IRA—simplified employee pension IRA—is an instrument specifically designed for small businesses.

A common question we get is whether your age matters, and for the most part, age is not a factor in terms of eligibility. Although your age can determine whether you can make additional contributions to a retirement account, it does not limit whether you can actually have a retirement account. For example, once you reach age 70½, you are no longer eligible to contribute additional money to an IRA. However, if you already have money in an IRA or 401(k), you can still roll that money over to a self-directed IRA or 401(k) anytime you want.

Many people are under the assumption that you need to have a job in order to have a self-directed retirement account. Again, not necessarily the case. Having earned income from W-2 or 1099 activities can affect how much you can contribute to a retirement account, but you can still have your own IRA or self-directed IRA even if you don't have a job. In addition, if your work provides you with a 401(k) account, you may still be able to open or contribute to a self-directed retirement account under many circumstances. You could even roll over 401(k) money from an old job into a self-directed account, regardless of your current occupation status.

On a similar note, you do not need to own a business or legal entity in order to have a self-directed retirement account. Certain accounts like IRAs or Roth IRAs are individual accounts and have nothing to do with a business or an employer. As long as you or your spouse have earned income, you may be eligible to have one of these retirement accounts.

Other retirement accounts such as a SEP-IRA, Solo 401(k), and a defined benefit plan do require earned income associated with a business. Keep in mind that this still does not necessarily mean you need to have a legal entity. For example, if you have a home-based business selling cosmetic products where you operate as a sole proprietor, that could allow you to be eligible for one of these more advanced business retirement accounts. A legal entity is not required.

Which Retirement Accounts Can Be Self-Directed?

Remember the only difference between a regular retirement account and self-directed retirement account is the type of assets your account is investing in, so here is a list of some common retirement accounts that can all be self-directed:

- Traditional IRA
- Roth IRA
- SEP-IRA
- Simple IRA
- Spousal IRA
- Inherited IRA
- Solo 401(k)
- Defined benefit plan

What if your financial planner told you that your money with Merrill Lynch can be self-directed? Does that mean you can leave your money there and use it to buy that investment property on Main Street? Probably not. Typically, when investment brokerage firms tell you that you can do "self-directed investing" in that account, they simply mean that you can choose the stocks, bonds, or mutual fund investments yourself. They generally are not going to allow you to put that money into a particular rental property that your retirement account will fully own. If you are truly looking to take control of your retirement money with self-directed investing, you need to have your retirement funds with an actual self-directed custodian.

As great as this powerful strategy can be, it does come with hidden traps and pitfalls. We will start with some basics of self-directed investing so that you can keep yourself out of trouble.

What Can a Self-Directed Retirement Account Invest In?

A self-directed retirement account can actually invest in almost anything. In fact, the IRS does not dictate what a retirement account can invest in; instead, the tax code tells us what we *cannot* invest in. Believe it or not, the list of items that you cannot invest in with your retirement account is incredibly short.

- *Collectibles*: Retirement accounts cannot be used to invest in collectibles. Collectibles include alcoholic beverages, stamps, gems, metals, antiques, rugs, and artwork. With respect to coins, an IRA is allowed to invest in one, one-half, one-quarter, or one-tenth ounce U.S. gold coins, or one-ounce silver coins minted by the Treasury Department. It can also invest in certain platinum coins and certain gold, silver, palladium, and platinum bullion.

- *Life Insurance*: A retirement account can be a beneficiary of a life insurance policy, but it cannot be on a title or be the owner of a life insurance policy. There is a small exception to this rule, but in general, life insurance is not an asset that your retirement account should purchase or invest in.
- *S Corporation Stock*: Retirement accounts cannot invest in S corporations. This actually has nothing to do with retirement account rules; instead, it is a limitation of S corporation tax rules. The IRS tax code for S corporations states that a retirement account cannot be a shareholder of an S corporation. However, retirement accounts can invest in many other entity types such as LLCs, partnerships, and C corporations.

Now that we know the short list of assets that retirement accounts cannot invest in, let's go through some common investments that can be done through a self-directed retirement account:

- Single family home
- Vacant lots
- Duplex, triplex, fourplex
- Apartment building
- Commercial shopping center
- Office building
- Mobile home parks
- Self-storage
- Promissory notes
- Businesses
- Start-up companies
- Cryptocurrency (like Bitcoin)
- Oil and gas investments
- REITs (real estate investment trusts)
- Syndicated deals (private placement offerings)
- LLC, partnership, or C corporation investments

If the type of asset you want to invest in is not on this list, don't fret! Remember, the list is not all encompassing. If it's not one of the three items you *cannot* invest in, there is a good possibility that it's available as an option. As always, check with your tax advisor before proceeding with any investment decisions.

Disqualified Persons and Prohibited Transactions

Self-directed investing provides a lot of flexibility, but before making an investment using your self-directed account, you need to understand some of the restrictions that the IRS imposes with respect to retirement investing. The IRS prohibits certain transactions from taking place when using retirement funds—commonly referred to as "prohibited transactions." Involvement in a prohibited transaction can be extremely costly and can result in some big tax and penalty bills.

What are these prohibited transactions, and how can we avoid them? On a high level, prohibited transactions are designed to ensure that your retirement money is not doing business with a disqualified person, such as yourself, certain people related to you, or your businesses.

Disqualified Persons

First and foremost, you as the retirement account owner are a disqualified person. Your spouse and your lineal ascendants and descendants are also disqualified persons to your retirement account, including your parents, grandparents, children, grandchildren, and adopted parents/children/grandchildren. Spouses of your children are also disqualified persons.

In addition to the people listed above, other disqualified persons include people providing services to the retirement plan—like your CPA, lawyer, self-directed custodian, financial advisor, and their employees. Any entities of which you (or those people listed above) own more than 50 percent are also a disqualified person.

Virtually any person or business not listed above should be able to transact with your retirement account without any tax issues. Many people are under the impression that all relatives are disqualified from your retirement, but that is actually not true. Reread that list of disqualified relatives above and see if you can guess who is missing! Here is a partial list of relatives who are not disqualified from your retirement account:

- Brothers and sisters
- Cousins

- Aunts and uncles
- Nieces and nephews
- Spouse's siblings
- In-laws

Prohibited Transactions

First of all, a disqualified person cannot sell, buy, or receive current benefit from assets in your retirement account. If you own a rental property already in your personal name, you cannot sell that property to your own retirement account. Since your mom is a disqualified person, this means she cannot sell a property to your retirement account. This works the same in the reverse: If your retirement account owns a rental property on Main Street, it cannot sell that property to you, your mom, or any other disqualified person. In addition, you can't sign contracts in your name and try to re-title assets into the retirement account at closing—the offer contract should be made in the name of the retirement account directly.

Now let's assume that your retirement account owns a rental property. If the toilet breaks and needs repairs, you can hire someone to fix the toilet. However, you cannot go there personally to fix the toilet. Your spouse, parents, and kids are also prohibited from going there to fix the toilet. Essentially, the rules indicate that disqualified people cannot provide any type of service to the retirement account asset—you cannot personally rehab the property, mow the lawn, or clean the pool. What if the rental in the retirement account needs to have the grass mowed and you want your kids to do that, and just not pay them? That is still a prohibited transaction. The IRS says that disqualified parties are not allowed to provide services to your retirement account asset whether they are paid or unpaid.

Another common prohibited transaction is the limitation on personal use of the asset. For example, if your retirement account owns the rental on Main Street, it means that you are not allowed to use that property. You cannot rent the house from your retirement account, and you cannot personally stay in that property. The same restrictions apply to the other people who are disqualified from your retirement account—if Main Street is an amazing vacation property, you and your kids cannot stay there while you are on vacation. However, your aunts and uncles are not disqualified parties, so they can stay in that property without creating any tax issues.

Loan transactions are also prohibited between disqualified parties, so you cannot lend money to or borrow money from your retirement account, and the account cannot be used as collateral for a personal loan. When your retirement account goes to borrow money, you cannot personally sign or guarantee that loan, either.

We all know that real estate investors are some of the most creative problem-solvers around. So, what if you decided to get "creative" to circumvent the rules? Since you cannot borrow money from your own IRA, what if you had your cousin borrow money from your IRA instead? Your cousin is not a disqualified person, so he is able to legitimately borrow money from your IRA with no tax issues. If your cousin turns around and lends you the money after borrowing it—unfortunately, the IRS is already on to that scheme. Your retirement account cannot use "others" to get around the prohibited transaction rules. The IRS looks at where the money started and where the money ended. In this case, the money ultimately went from the retirement account back to you, and thus, it is a prohibited transaction.

Make sure that you do not pay retirement account expenses with your personal funds or pay personal expenses with retirement funds. Keep retirement money separate from your personal or business funds so the IRS does not try to classify these as distributions or prohibited transactions.

Committing a prohibited transaction can be an extremely costly mistake. If a retirement account does get involved in one of these prohibited transactions, the account can be canceled and immediately become subject to taxes and certain penalties. Note that the *entire* value of your retirement account could be subject to taxes and penalties, not just the value of the prohibited investment.

If you committed a prohibited transaction by lending $10,000 to your mom, and you also have $100,000 invested in a typical mutual fund, the IRS could close the retirement account and assess taxes and penalties on the entire $110,000 of assets in the account. This is definitely not something you want to happen, so if you are ever unsure as to whether something is a prohibited transaction, we recommend that you consult with your team of advisors before taking that next step.

WHAT DOES IT ALL MEAN?

In this chapter, we have discussed what self-directed retirement account investing means. We've covered who can have a self-directed account along with which types of accounts can be self-directed. We've also discussed the type of assets a retirement account can invest in, which ones it cannot invest in, and which investments you should avoid with disqualified people.

It is easy to open a self-directed account and virtually anyone can have one. Make sure that you work with your tax advisor, as well as a self-directed custodian, before making any investment decisions. When in doubt, double-check a proposed transaction with your team of advisors to make sure it is done correctly.

With great power comes great responsibility, and in self-directed investing, you are in full control and thus solely responsible for avoiding prohibited transactions. A good CPA or custodian will try to help if they see you heading down the wrong path, but at the end of the day, it's your responsibility. When a self-directed investment is used incorrectly, violating any of the prohibited transactions could be an extremely costly mistake when taxes and penalties are assessed. But when used correctly, self-directed investing can be an extremely powerful tool that can supercharge your real estate investing and your retirement planning!

CHAPTER 11
BIGGER AND BETTER RETIREMENT ACCOUNTS

"Someone's sitting in the shade today because someone planted a tree a long time ago."

—WARREN BUFFETT

Self-directed investing allows us to combine the benefits of tax-advantaged growth with our expertise in real estate to grow our wealth faster. The synergy of tax benefits and real estate investing should be part of any investor's wealth-building plan.

The first major tax benefit of self-directed investing is that when you make contributions into a retirement account, you reduce your tax bill in that current year. The second benefit is that the money in the retirement account can then grow on a tax-deferred basis. Every year, 100 percent of the income generated by that asset continues to grow tax-deferred, and none of that is paid to the government until you take the money out of the retirement account. If you are in the higher tax brackets, retirement contribution can reduce your taxes by close to 50 percent—a very significant amount of tax savings each year.

You are probably familiar with IRAs and 401(k)s. Individual retirement accounts (IRAs) were created back in the mid-seventies and have been popular ever since. These are the accounts in which you can typically contribute around $6,000 per year to grow tax-deferred. Commonly provided by employers, 401(k) accounts allow you to make contributions each year, and your employer may also make some contributions to help you save for your retirement.

You may not know, however, that there are a handful of bigger and better retirement accounts available to help save even more on taxes. Let's take a quick refresher on the more common traditional IRA and Roth IRA first, and then we'll dive into the sexier retirement accounts. (Yes, taxes and retirement planning can be sexy!)

Individual Retirement Account (IRA)

Whether an individual retirement account is a regular IRA or a self-directed IRA, both are fairly easy to set up and maintain. Contributions made into an IRA are generally tax-deductible. If you contributed $6,000 into your IRA, your taxable income may be decreased by $6,000 this year.

In addition to the current year tax savings, earnings generated within the IRA generally grow tax-deferred—the profits are not taxed each year, so there is compounded growth within the IRA. Instead, you defer the taxes over multiple years and only pay taxes when you withdraw the money at some point in the future. The deadline for making contributions can be as late as April 15 of the following tax year. The benefit here is that, oftentimes, you can wait until your tax returns are done before deciding whether you want to contribute to your IRA to reduce last year's taxes.

Although you need to have earned income in order to make contributions for that year, there is no income requirement to open an IRA. For example, if you retired last year and accumulated some money in your old employer 401(k), you can roll that money into an IRA this year, even if you made no income at all. You also can contribute to an IRA even with no income as long as your spouse earned income in that particular year.

There are some disadvantages to the IRA, however. One of the main limitations is the amount of contribution that can be made each year. The annual contributions are typically limited to $6,000 per year for those under age 50. Plus, once you reach age 70½, you can no longer make additional contributions into the IRA, and rules kick in regarding required minimum distributions (RMDs), which means that every year you must withdraw a certain amount of money from the retirement account, regardless of whether you need or want that money.

This does not mean you must wait until age 70½ to take money out of your IRA. In fact, you can take money out of your IRA anytime you want. Taking money out once you reach retirement age simply means that the distributions taken out become taxable in that year. However, if you take money out of your IRA before you reach the age of 59½, the money may also be subject to early distribution penalties.

Roth IRA

A Roth IRA is also an individual retirement account and functions very similar to a traditional IRA. The main difference is that with the Roth IRA, your contributions to the account are not tax-deductible. Instead, the money in the Roth IRA grows tax-free forever, as long as it stays in the Roth IRA.

For example, if you contributed $6,000 into your Roth IRA this year, it would not reduce your current income taxes. Let's say that you take the $6,000 and invest it in an asset that generates cash flow and appreciation. As long as the earnings are kept within the Roth IRA, there are no taxes due. If, by the end of seven years, that $6,000 of Roth IRA money grows to be $20,000, all of that growth is tax-free. When you decide to take some or all of that $20,000 out of the Roth IRA, the distribution can potentially be tax-free as well.

A regular Roth IRA and a self-directed Roth IRA are both fairly easy to set up and maintain. The deadline for making contributions can be as late as April 15 of the following tax year, and similar to the IRA, Roth IRA contributions can only be made in years where you or your spouse have earned income. While the IRA has required minimum distributions when retirement age is reached, the added benefit of your Roth IRA is that there are generally no required minimum distributions. If your Roth IRA has $100,000, you can choose to leave that money in the account to continue to grow tax-free, even after you reach the age of 70½. If you lived until you were 99 years old, the Roth could have an additional 29-plus years of completely tax-free growth. If you passed away with all that money in your Roth IRA, wouldn't that be an amazing gift to leave to your kids and grandkids?

Unlike the traditional IRA, though, Roth IRA contributions are only available to taxpayers under certain income limitations. As with many things in the tax world, there are strategies to get around the Roth limitation, like the backdoor Roth IRA conversion.

The Backdoor Roth IRA Plan

Suzy was a marketing manager with a high W-2 income. She maximized her 401(k) at work every year in order to save for retirement. Suzy never had any regular or Roth IRAs in the past and only contributed to her work 401(k). She loved the idea of setting aside some money in a Roth account to grow completely tax-free toward retirement. However, because her income every year exceeded the IRS limitation, she previously had never been allowed to put money into a Roth IRA. To get around this hurdle, Suzy implemented the backdoor Roth IRA plan. The plan takes a few steps:

STEP 1: OPEN AND FUND A TRADITIONAL IRA.

Suzy opened an IRA account and made a non-deductible contribution of $6,000. Because of Suzy's high income, she would not receive any tax savings by making contributions into a regular IRA.

STEP 2: OPEN A ROTH IRA ACCOUNT.

After money was in the traditional IRA account, Suzy could then open a new Roth IRA account, either with the same custodian or with a different custodian. Because Suzy's income was over the IRS limit, she could not make any contributions directly into the Roth IRA.

STEP 3: CONVERT MONEY FROM THE REGULAR IRA TO THE ROTH IRA.

This step is very simple, and it just means transferring money from the IRA account into the Roth IRA account. Although the IRS has limitations on who can make contributions into a Roth IRA, there are no income limitations on who can "convert" money from a regular IRA into a Roth IRA. Since Suzy had $6,000 in a traditional IRA, she could convert it to her new Roth IRA anytime she wanted.

After Suzy moved the $6,000 from her regular IRA into her Roth IRA, the money grew tax-free permanently in the Roth IRA. Since Suzy did not receive a tax deduction when she put the original $6,000 into the IRA, she did not owe taxes when she "converted" that money into her Roth IRA account. This strategy can actually be utilized each and every year. In a few years, Suzy could be sitting on a large pile of money that is growing completely tax-free inside her Roth IRA.

As we discussed previously, both IRAs and Roth IRAs can be self-directed into real estate and other alternative investments—they are not locked into the stock market and mutual funds. However, there are several other types of retirement accounts that can be even more powerful than the IRAs because they allow for more flexibility, higher contributions, and more investment options.

Solo 401(k)

While having your own business is not necessary to obtain a self-directed retirement account, people who do have their own businesses are able to contribute more to their retirement accounts each year. Higher contribution limits and additional flexibility can be achieved with accounts such as the Solo 401(k), otherwise known as the Individual 401(k) or Qualified Retirement Plan (QRP).

Bill and Patricia: Solo 401(k) Success

Bill and his wife, Patricia, had built a successful real estate brokerage business in California over the past few years. A couple of agents worked under them, but none were W-2 employees. Their brokerage business operated as a sole proprietorship, and every year they netted around $370,000 in profits. As their income increased the past few years, their taxes also increased significantly. Bill and Patricia didn't feel as if they received any proactive tax planning advice from their tax preparer and suspected that there was more they could do to save on taxes.

Every year, their tax preparer would advise that they each contribute $6,000 into an IRA, which was apparently their only option for retirement contributions because of their high income. At a federal and state tax rate of 41 percent, the $12,000 IRA contribution saved them $4,920 in income taxes. Not a bad amount of savings, but as we're sure you would agree, not that significant either.

When we started working with Bill and Patricia, one of the strategies we helped to implement was the Solo 401(k). As a sole proprietorship, Bill and Patricia were the owners—as well as employees—of their business. With a Solo 401(k), contributions can be made by both the employer and the employee, and both can be tax-deductible. As employees of their sole proprietorship, Bill and Patricia can each make an employee contribution into their Solo 401(k) of $19,000. This means that between the two of them, they can make total combined employee contributions of $38,000 into their Solo 401(k) to reduce taxes for the year. Based on their tax rate of 41 percent, this would save them $15,580 in taxes.

Because the Solo 401(k) is a business retirement account, the sole proprietorship can also make retirement contributions for Bill and Patricia. As the employer, the business can fund an additional 20 percent of contributions based on the business's net profit—an additional $37,000 each into retirement for Bill and Patricia. This could result in total employer Solo(k) contributions of $74,000, and at their tax rate of 41 percent, could save them $30,340 in taxes.

Between employer and employee contributions, Bill and Patricia might be able to save over $45,000 in taxes just using this single tax strategy. Let's look at a side-by-side comparison to see how much Bill and Patricia might save in taxes using an IRA versus a Solo 401(k):

	Traditional IRA	Solo 401(K)	Difference
Retirement Plan Contribution	$12,000	$112,000	**$100,000**
Tax Rate	41%	41%	
Total Tax Savings	$4,920	$45,920	**$41,000**

As you can see, not only would Bill and Patricia be able to save an additional $41,000 in taxes by using the Solo 401(k), they would also be able to contribute an additional $100,000 to grow tax-deferred for their retirement. That $100,000 could be used to purchase a rental property inside the Solo 401(k), and all the cash flow and appreciation could grow tax-deferred for them for many more years.

Solo 401(k) Advantages
There are several advantages that the Solo 401(k) has over the IRA or Roth IRA—one is the higher contribution limits. With a Solo 401(k), there are two buckets: the employee bucket and the employer bucket. With the employee bucket, the owner/employee can make contributions of up

to $19,000 per year. This is the same type of contributions that you can make if you were working at a job and you participated in your work 401(k) plan.

The employer bucket is where the business makes a contribution into your retirement account to help you save for the future. If the business operates as a sole proprietorship, the maximum profit-sharing contribution the business can make is based on 20 percent of the business net profits. If the business is operating as an S corporation with which the owner is receiving a W-2 from that business, then the maximum profit-sharing contribution the business could make would be 25 percent of the owner's W-2 wages.

When you combine the employer bucket and the employee bucket, the maximum annual amount that can be contributed is up to $56,000 per person. If you have married taxpayers who both work in the business, that could be $112,000 per year, which is much more powerful than saving just $6,000 toward retirement each year.

One of the limitations of most retirement accounts is that once the money is in there, the only way to access the cash is to take distributions. If you have money in an IRA or a Roth IRA, you are not able to borrow from those accounts if you need to use those funds for personal items. However, with a Solo 401(k), you are actually allowed to borrow money.

Let's say that after making contributions into their Solo 401(k), Bill and Patricia realized that they needed to access some of that cash to use for their daughter's wedding. By taking a loan from their Solo 401(k), Bill and Patricia could access their retirement money and use it for personal needs, all on a tax-free and penalty-free basis.

For the Solo 401(k) loan, you can borrow up to the lesser of 50 percent of the account balance or $50,000. For example, if your Solo 401(k) had $80,000 in it, you could borrow up to $40,000. If it had $150,000 in it, the maximum you could borrow would be $50,000.

Many people are under the impression that Solo 401(k) loans can only be used for certain things. However, you are actually able to borrow the money for any reason you want. It could be to pay for college, pay for a wedding, or simply go on vacation. Of course, if you wanted to borrow from your Solo 401(k) to invest in a rental or buy a primary home, that would be allowable as well. When you borrow from your Solo 401(k), you need to have a written loan document in place and make loan repayments at least every quarter. The maximum loan period can be five years, and each loan payment would include principal and interest.

Another advantage of the Solo 401(k) is that it allows additional time to make contributions into the retirement account. As we discussed, the deadline for making a contribution to an IRA or a Roth IRA is April 15 of the year following the tax year that the contribution relates to. This is the deadline, even if your taxes are on extension with the IRS. However, with a Solo 401(k), you have until the date you file the employer's tax return in order to make that contribution. If your business is an S corporation and you file an extension for that tax return, the due date for that return will be September 15. If you wait until September 15 to file the S corporation tax return, you can contribute to your Solo 401(k) as late as September 15. If you filed the S corporation tax return on September 1, then September 1 would be the last day to make the retirement contributions.

Similarly, if your business files taxes as a sole proprietorship, you could have until October 15 to make your Solo 401(k) contribution, provided your personal taxes are on extension with the IRS. If cash flow or liquidity is an issue for you, you can have an extra five to six months to gather up the funds to contribute to your Solo 401(k) as compared to an IRA.

It is important to note that, while you have an extended deadline for making the contribution to your Solo 401(k), you generally have to set up the Solo 401(k) by December 31 of the tax year in question. If you want to utilize the Solo 401(k) strategy to reduce taxes for the 2020 year, you need to set up the account by December 31, 2020. You would then have until the date you file the business's tax return in 2021 to actually fund the account.

Even though the Solo 401(k) is sometimes referred to as the "Individual 401(k)," if you have a business for which your spouse also works, then your spouse would also be eligible to participate in the Solo 401(k) plan. Depending on how much income your spouse earns from this business, they may also be able to maximize their contributions into their Solo 401(k) account. This is exactly what we saw in Bill and Patricia's case; because both Bill and Patricia worked in their real estate brokerage business, both were able to contribute to their Solo 401(k) to reduce their total taxes.

Another advantage that the Solo 401(k) has over an IRA or a Roth IRA is its ability to invest in leveraged real estate and be able to avoid a hidden tax known as UDFI tax. UDFI refers to Unrelated Debt Financed Income. We'll dive into it more in the next chapter, but the gist is that your retirement account may have to pay taxes each year on taxable profit that is related to debt. For example, if your retirement account bought a property for $100,000 using $50,000 as a down payment and obtained a $50,000 mortgage, then 50 percent of the property is debt-financed. If in the first year, that property makes a net taxable profit of $5,000, then 50 percent of that profit could be subject to this UDFI tax.

As mentioned, we'll go into this in more detail in the next chapter. Many investors are unaware of this hidden tax, which applies to almost every type of retirement account. The Solo 401(k) can invest in leveraged real estate and is not subject to UDFI taxes, another huge advantage.

Who Can Have a Solo 401(k)?

You must have a business in order to have a Solo 401(k), so you must be self-employed. In addition, you need to receive compensation or "earned income" from the business. If you operate as a sole proprietorship, earned income is simply the income that your sole proprietorship generates. If you operate in a legal entity such as an S corporation or a C corporation, the W-2 income you pay yourself could be eligible for Solo 401(k) contributions. Active income earned via an LLC or a partnership may be eligible for Solo 401(k) contributions as well. If you are in the business of wholesaling or flipping real estate deals, then you may be eligible to have a Solo 401(k). However, income from interest, dividends, capital gains, and rental income are *not* eligible for Solo 401(k) contributions—so if the only activity of a business is rental income, then it would not be eligible to have a Solo 401(k).

Another limitation of the Solo 401(k) is that the employees of the business can only be the owners and their spouses. There is an exception to this rule, however. If you have other W-2 employees in your business but they all work less than 1,000 hours per year, then you may still be eligible.

A common question we get is whether you need to have a legal entity in order to have a Solo 401(k), and the answer is no. You can have a Solo 401(k) even if you don't have a legal entity. You also don't actually need a net profit—if you are a sole proprietor property manager, you can open a Solo 401(k) even if your business generated a net loss for the year. However, in order to make additional contributions into the Solo 401(k), you do need to have net annual profit, because your contribution amount is calculated based on a percentage of the business's profit. If your business is taxed as an S corporation or as a C corporation, though, then the business's net profit (or lack thereof) is irrelevant. In this case, the amount that could be contributed to your Solo 401(k) would be dictated by the amount of W-2 compensation you receive from the corporation.

Now that you understand the tax benefits and eligibility requirements of the Solo 401(k) retirement account, we want to share with you an even more powerful option:

Defined Benefit Plan

Elaine, a 56-year-old attorney, had developed a successful law practice that generated an annual net profit of $250,000. She had a few part-time employees who would help her during the busy season, but no one worked for her full-time. Elaine had been contributing to her Solo 401(k) for years, but she wanted to set aside even more money than what the Solo 401(k) allowed.

When we found out that Elaine wanted to maximize retirement funds and reduce her current taxes, we discussed the possibility of achieving both of those goals using a defined benefit plan. Though she was familiar with the usual small business retirement plan options—like the SEP-IRA and Solo 401(k)—she had not heard of the defined benefit plan before.

In our first year of working with Elaine, she was able to set up a defined benefit plan and contribute over $100,000. At her combined federal and state tax rate of 45 percent, the contribution saved her $45,000 in taxes that year, plus she had another $100,000 in her retirement account growing on a tax-deferred basis.

What Is a Defined Benefit Plan?

A defined benefit plan is an employer-sponsored retirement plan in which contributions are made by the employer to reduce the current year's taxes due. Similar to the Solo 401(k), a legal entity is not required to establish a defined benefit plan, but you do need to have earned income from self-employment activities. Money contributed into the Defined Benefit Plan reduces current taxes and grows tax-deferred until it is distributed at retirement age. Similar to the Solo 401(k), a defined benefit plan can also be self-directed into assets such as real estate. If Elaine wanted to, the $100,000 in her defined benefit plan could be used to purchase a rental or invest in other alternative assets that are not prohibited by the IRS.

So how is it possible that Elaine could use a defined benefit plan to put in such a large contribution? The answer is based on how defined benefit plan contributions are calculated. Unlike a 401(k) plan, which defines the amount of contribution you make, a defined benefit plan starts with the end goal in mind. Defined benefit plan contribution amounts are based on actuarial calculations to determine what your retirement benefit would be, and then the calculations figure out what you need to contribute today in order to arrive at your goal. It establishes a predetermined monthly benefit amount at retirement.

This means that the older you are, the higher your potential contributions are each year. In the calculation of a defined benefit plan, you are trying to arrive at a specified benefit amount at retirement age. As such, the closer you are to retirement age, the higher the potential contributions—so a defined benefit plan can be much more powerful for someone in their 50s than someone in their 30s.

An ideal profile for defined benefit plans would be for a business whose owners are 50 years or older. If the business has other employees, the plan works best when the employees are in their 20s and 30s. And if you want to know exactly how much your monthly retirement check will be, then a defined benefit plan may be a good tool.

Believe it or not, this plan can be used in conjunction with a Solo 401(k) in the same year. In Elaine's example, just because she contributed to her new defined benefit plan, this didn't mean that her Solo 401(k) contributions had to be eliminated. In fact, she was also able to continue maxing out her Solo 401(k) contributions each year. Between her Solo 401(k) and her defined benefit plan, Elaine decided to put away $162,000 into retirement accounts for that year. The money will grow tax-deferred, and she received an annual tax savings of close to $73,000. What a great way for Elaine to supersize her tax savings and also supercharge her retirement wealth!

WHAT DOES IT ALL MEAN?

As business owners, we are no longer limited to the few thousands of dollars for IRA and Roth IRA contributions. The tax code is filled with benefits where businesses can stash away $50,000 to $100,000 or more in money each year toward retirement. If you are a business that wants to reduce taxes and have more tax-advantaged growing money, make sure to strategize with your tax advisor on the benefits of self-directed Solo 401(k)s.

This type of plan provides you with much higher contribution amounts, flexibility to borrow, and flexibility to take on outside loans. Just like most other types of retirement accounts, Solo 401(k)s can be self-directed into real estate and other alternative assets. If you are hungry for more, consider the use of a defined benefit plan to further supercharge your retirement investing and take your tax reduction strategy to another level.

CHAPTER 12

TWO RETIREMENT INVESTING TAX TRAPS AND HOW TO AVOID THEM

"By failing to prepare, you are preparing to fail."

—**BENJAMIN FRANKLIN**

One of the most amazing benefits of investing inside a retirement account is the tax-advantaged growth. When a pretax retirement account invests in an asset and earns a return, you as the account owner do not usually have to pay taxes on that money until you withdraw from the account. This means that 100 percent of the earnings continue to grow year after year without any of it going to the IRS. If it is a Roth retirement account, that's even better—the asset grows tax-free, and you never pay taxes on it.

What many people may not know is that the IRS can assess taxes on investment assets even if they remain within your retirement account. We understand this sounds ridiculous, but unfortunately, that is the current tax law. Taxes are often assessed for investors who use retirement funds for real estate. There are two hidden tax traps that you should know about when it comes to investing in alternative assets with your retirement money: The first is referred to as the Unrelated Business Income Tax (UBIT), and the second is the Unrelated Debt Financed Income (UDFI) tax. We will cover both of these hidden tax traps, as well as disclose strategies that may help minimize or eliminate these taxes.

What Is UBIT, and How Does It Impact Real Estate Investors?

As we mentioned, most retirement accounts grow tax-deferred as long as you keep the money in the retirement account—this is because the government wanted to incentivize people to save for retirement. Generally, retirement accounts will invest in assets that create investment income, like rents, interest, dividends, and capital gains from selling stocks or mutual funds.

However, what if you want to use self-directed investing to generate other types of income that are not investment-related? For example, what if you want to use your retirement money to buy a McDonald's franchise? The McDonald's franchise will make a profit selling hamburgers, and all of that profit can go back into your self-directed retirement account. Although the IRS allows you to use retirement money to invest in a McDonald's franchise, there is a hidden tax that is associated with this particular investment.

This is where the unrelated business income tax (UBIT) comes in. Essentially, the IRS would impose this tax on your retirement account because the income earned from selling hamburgers is considered ordinary income of a business operation and not investment income (such as rents, interest, dividends). Selling hamburgers is an ordinary business activity, and thus the UBIT tax could apply. If your cousin owns a start-up technology business that sells online apps, your retirement account *can* invest in that business, but it may be subject to UBIT taxes.

To find out whether a particular investment will be subject to UBIT taxes, ask yourself this question: *Will my retirement account earn ordinary income or investment income?* If the answer is ordinary income, then UBIT will generally apply.

What, then, is "ordinary" income? It is essentially any income that is not investment income. If your retirement account invested in a business that sells widgets, provides services, or manufactures products, that is likely considered ordinary income. With respect to real estate, the three most common examples of ordinary income that could potentially be subject to UBIT taxes are fix-and-flip income, wholesale income, and development income. These three types of income are treated as ordinary income for income tax purposes and thus fall within the definitions of income that may be subject to UBIT taxes.

Don't "Flip" Out: A Solution to UBIT Taxes

Joey owns a handful of rentals but focuses mostly on fix-and-flips. He has a system for finding underperforming properties and knows how to create value by fixing them up. Joey learned about self-directed investing through his local real estate network and was excited to get started right away. His CPA is not well versed in self-directed investing, but Joey doesn't think that will be a problem at all. After all, isn't retirement account money already tax-advantaged? What could go wrong?

Joey works with a self-directed custodian and sets up a self-directed Solo 401(k). He has done a tax-free trustee-to-trustee rollover of his old IRA funds into his new self-directed 401(k) and has purchased a property to flip. Based on what he learned from other investors, Joey knew he needed to hire contractors and other service providers to do the rehab work because he could not do any of the rehab himself.

After just two months, his flip property sold for a $20,000 gain. He made more money in those two months in his retirement account than what it had earned in the last five years being invested in mutual funds! Joey did not waste any time and quickly moved his retirement money into more flip deals. By the end of the year, Joey's self-directed 401(k) had flipped five properties and made over $65,000 in profit.

However, when it was time for Joey to file his tax returns, he finally learned about UBIT. After some research, his CPA learned that fix-and-flip profit is considered ordinary income and, as such, is subject to UBIT taxes of up to 37 percent. After all was said and done, Joey's 401(k) owed the IRS close to $24,000 in taxes for that year. The additional bad news is that, once Joey retires and takes this money out of his retirement account, he will still need to pay taxes on the distribution.

Had Joey done some proactive planning or found a tax advisor who had experience with self-directed investing, he would have known about the high UBIT taxes that would be assessed on his flip properties. As we've seen before with taxes, there are ways to avoid this pitfall—some can be accomplished with simple changes in the way a deal is structured.

For example, what if instead of flipping properties in his 401(k), he lent money to other flip investors?

As a lender, your 401(k) could earn interest, fees, and origination points—and the income your 401(k) earns is considered interest income. As discussed previously, interest income is considered investment income in the eyes of the IRS and thus avoids UBIT taxes. This is the case even if your 401(k) is lending money to someone in the flipping business. Do be careful, though, that the interest you charge is reasonable and allowable under lending rules. If part of the return earned by your 401(k) loan is a profit split from the flip deal, that portion can still be subject to UBIT taxes.

Another potential way to avoid UBIT taxes on fix-and-flip real estate is to turn the property into a BRRRR property. Instead of selling the property right away, what if Joey's self-directed 401(k) held on to the property and rented it out for a period of time? That would give Joey a few options:

- **Option 1:** His 401(k) could rent it out and hold the property long term.
- **Option 2:** His 401(k) could rent it out and then refinance to take out equity from the property. Then the 401(k) could use the equity to purchase another investment property.
- **Option 3:** His 401(k) could rent it out and then sell after renting for over a year.

Using this strategy, Joey would be able to turn his flip property into a rental property for tax purposes. Should Joey decide to sell the property down the road, the profit would be considered capital gains income, which is also considered investment income and thus escapes UBIT taxes as well.

Another potential strategy is to show that the intention was to hold the property as a rental and not a flip. Even if a property is purchased, rehabbed, and sold fairly quickly, if you can demonstrate that you intended to keep the property as a rental, then your retirement account may be able to avoid UBIT taxes.

Let's assume that Joey originally planned to purchase, rehab, and keep the property as a rental. Let's also assume that, during the rehab process, the city created a new law that imposed rent control on this property. Based on the new rent control rules, Joey would have a property with negative cash flow if he held on to it. By selling the property because of the new rent control change, Joey might be able to avoid UBIT taxes under the argument that his plan was to keep it as a rental. This is an extremely subjective area of the tax law, so if your plan is to try to avoid UBIT taxes using your "rental intention" as your case, make sure to plan proactively with your tax advisor to ensure that you indeed meet all the criteria and have the appropriate documentation to support your argument.

What Is UDFI, and How Does It Impact Real Estate Investors?

Unrelated debt financed income (UDFI) is a subset of UBIT. When certain types of retirement accounts invest in an asset that has unrelated debt-financed income, the retirement account may need to pay the UBIT tax based on the amount of UDFI. We understand this is confusing, so we will simply refer to them as UDFI taxes.

The UDFI tax is assessed when a retirement account invests in an asset that also uses leverage, or money the retirement account has borrowed. In other words, whenever debt is involved in a retirement account investment, you should look into whether UDFI taxes will apply. Since most real estate investors utilize leverage in their deals, UDFI taxes are a hidden issue that impacts many who use self-directed investing to buy rental properties.

Although the IRS allows your retirement account to invest using leverage, the agency does not want the leveraged portion of that investment to also receive tax-advantaged growth. Let's assume your self-directed IRA has $40,000 in the account. The self-directed IRA obtains a $60,000 loan to purchase a $100,000 rental property. The IRS feels that the portion of the investment made from your retirement funds should grow tax-advantaged. In this case, 40 percent of the asset would be associated with funds from your retirement account, so 40 percent of the profit should grow tax-advantaged. However, 60 percent of this investment was purchased with a loan and not with retirement funds. As such, 60 percent of the profit should not receive tax-advantaged growth.

Unfortunately, the calculation of UDFI taxes is extremely complex, so this is definitely not something you want to tackle using an off-the-shelf software. To demonstrate with a simplified version of the calculation, if this rental property generated $20,000 of income during the year, then 60 percent of it could be taxable—so $12,000 of the rental income could be taxed at a rate of up to 37 percent. The taxes could be roughly $4,000.

It is important to note that UDFI taxes are not related to income taxes at all. Just because your retirement account pays UDFI taxes, it does not mean that future distributions from that retirement account will be tax-free. You may still need to pay income taxes in the future when you take the earnings out of the retirement account as distributions, so part of the income can be taxed twice by the government.

The UDFI tax can be an issue when retirement money invests in an asset with leverage. These taxes may apply in all of the following situations:

- Your retirement account purchases a single-family home with a mortgage.
- Your retirement account is a passive investor in a syndication LLC that takes out a loan to buy a property.
- Your retirement account purchases a property with all cash but later takes out a loan in a refinance.

Since real estate investors love to utilize leverage, UDFI is a potential problem in many transactions, but there are ways to minimize or even avoid them altogether.

Avoid Debt

The first and easiest strategy is to avoid the use of debt in your retirement account investments. Instead of purchasing an expensive property, consider investing in a lower-priced property with sufficient cash in your retirement account to purchase it without any financing. If your self-directed IRA does not have enough to purchase the property, maybe you can roll over funds from other retirement accounts into your self-directed IRA to increase the total funds available. For example, if you have money laying around in a 401(k) from your work or from a previous employer, consider rolling the 401(k) money over into your self-directed IRA and then use that money to purchase a property with all cash.

Another potential strategy to avoid debt is to take on equity investors. If you want to purchase a $100,000 property but only have $60,000 in your retirement account, you can find another investor to partner with your IRA to make the purchase. Your partner can fund the remaining $40,000 to purchase the property, so there is no leverage on the retirement account investment and UDFI taxes would not apply.

If you aren't able to avoid debt in your self-directed IRA investments, one way to lessen the tax hit is to reduce the debt as much as you can. For example, if your investment started out with 80 percent of the property as debt, then 80 percent of the taxable income would be subject to the high UDFI taxes. However, if you paid that debt down to 50 percent, then only 50 percent of the taxable income may be subject to UDFI taxes. The actual calculation is a bit more complex in its details, but for simplicity's sake, you can see how paying down the debt can help significantly reduce the UDFI taxes.

Investing Through a Self-Directed Solo 401(k)

What if you do not have enough funds to buy an all-cash property and also do not have anyone you want to partner with? Another strategy to avoid UDFI taxes is to invest in leveraged real estate through a self-directed Solo 401(k). One of the benefits that the Solo 401(k) has over an IRA is that the IRS allows the Solo 401(k) to invest in leveraged real estate and pay no UDFI taxes. Even if your Solo 401(k) invests in a rental property that is 90 percent leveraged, all of the return on that investment grows in a tax-advantaged matter within the Solo 401(k). None of it is subject to UDFI taxes. It is important to keep in mind, however, that this only applies to acquisition loans incurred with respect to the purchase of the property.

Does it sound too good to be true? We are not sure why this loophole exists for Solo 401(k)s, but regardless of the reason, it is a great benefit that can help you invest in leveraged real estate and avoid UDFI taxes completely. Remember, though—not everyone is eligible for a Solo 401(k). If you need a refresher, look back to the previous chapter to see if you would be eligible for this type of retirement account.

Tax Offset Strategies

Yet another way to reduce UDFI taxes when investing in leveraged real estate is to look at the traditional strategies that apply to real estate taxes. The UDFI tax is assessed on taxable income from the investment, so the best way to minimize the tax is to reduce the total taxable income.

Let's assume that you purchased a rental property in your self-directed IRA for $200,000, with a 40 percent down payment and a bank loan for the remaining $120,000. In this scenario, your IRA investment is 60 percent leveraged.

Loan: $120,000 (60%)

Down payment: $80,000 (40%)

Purchase price: $200,000 (100%)

Now let's assume that the property generated $13,000 of rental income and had interest, taxes, and other expenses of $9,000. In addition, the property has depreciation expenses of $5,800. This creates a total net loss for tax purposes, so there would be no UDFI taxes due for that year.

Rental income: $13,000

Rental expenses: –$9,000

Depreciation: –$5,800

Total tax loss: –$1,800

As you can see, one of the ways to reduce UDFI taxes is to increase deductions. Whether the deductions are from operating expenses such as interest, taxes, and management fees or from tax items like depreciation, these can all help to reduce or eliminate UDFI taxes. You can even combine this strategy with the cost segregation strategy we discussed in Chapter 2 to supercharge your tax savings. If a cost segregation increases your depreciation to $23,000 this year and the property's rental income was $20,000, a cost segregation may a good strategy to wipe out the taxable income and eliminate UDFI taxes.

Without Cost Segregation		With Cost Segregation	
Rental Income	$20,000	Rental Income	$20,000
Rental Expenses	($9,000)	Rental Expenses	($9,000)
Depreciation	($5,800)	Accelerated Depreciation	($23,000)
Total Tax Income	$5,200	Total Tax Loss	($12,000)

A similar strategy can be helpful when selling a rental property that has debt. When a leveraged property within an IRA is sold, the capital gains allocated to the leveraged portion are also subject to UDFI taxes. If the property is 60 percent leveraged, the IRA may need to pay capital gains taxes on 60 percent of the gain in that year. One creative strategy may be to consider implementing a 1031 exchange within the IRA—just like a regular 1031 exchange, an exchange within a self-directed IRA could mean there is no taxable income and thus no UDFI taxes.

Any investment losses from previous tax years can be carried forward to offset future UDFI income from taxes, too. If your IRA had taxable income this year but also had some unused UDFI losses from previous years related to that property, you could use those losses to offset your current year UDFI income. For example, let's assume that your leveraged rental property generated some tax losses for the first three years, and in Year 4, your IRA sells the property for a taxable gain. Those losses from the first three years can be carried forward to now reduce the taxes on the capital gains in your IRA.

Why Is This Tax Missed by So Many Investors?

The UBIT and UDFI taxes can be assessed on most types of retirement accounts. You may be surprised to learn that these taxes also apply to Roth accounts. Even though a Roth IRA or Roth Solo 401(k) is completely tax-free, it can still be subject to UBIT taxes just like the other pretax retirement accounts.

The vast majority of investors do not know about these hidden taxes. A large number of tax advisors do not understand self-directed investing, so it's not surprising to learn that an even larger percentage of advisors are not aware of UDFI and UBIT taxes, either. If your tax advisor has not heard of these taxes, then how could you have known about them?

Let's say that you learned about self-directed investing last year. You move your money into a self-directed account and invest in an apartment syndication. The apartment syndication uses investors' money as the down payment and obtains a bank loan for the remainder, and that leverage means that your retirement account is subject to UDFI taxes. The following April, you meet with your tax preparer to do last year's taxes, and during the discussion, you mention that you invested in an apartment syndication. Your tax preparer asks you some questions and finds out that your retirement account made the investment.

If your tax preparer is not well versed in self-directed investing rules, they would likely tell you that they do not need to see your paperwork. They don't need to report the income from that apartment investment on your personal tax return because it's not *your* income. It's income earned by your retirement account, and that money grows tax-advantaged in the retirement account. You personally pay no taxes on the profit now, and you only pay taxes on that money when you take it out at retirement.

What they say would be correct. Retirement account income is not reported on your personal tax returns, and you personally do not pay taxes on UBIT—instead, UBIT taxes are reported on Form 990-T and are filed completely separate from your personal tax returns. In fact, the IRS requires that the UBIT and UDFI taxes that your retirement account owes need to be paid from the retirement account and not from your personal bank account.

So how do you know if you need to worry about these taxes? The best way is to communicate with your tax advisor before making any investments with your self-directed retirement account. If you are considering an investment that involves a mortgage—or if you are investing in real estate or a business that may earn ordinary income rather than investment income—it's a good idea to speak with your tax advisor beforehand.

If you have already made an investment in your self-directed retirement account, take the paperwork to your tax advisor at tax time. This way, they can help you determine whether UBIT or UDFI taxes apply. If your tax advisor is not familiar with self-directed investing, then take the time to interview others who have more experience in this area.

Are UBIT or UDFI Necessarily Bad?

Obviously, nobody likes to pay taxes if they don't have to, and that includes retirement money, too. We have discussed some ways that retirement funds can structure deals differently to minimize or avoid the hidden UBIT and UDFI taxes. However, the strategies may not work in all situations. If you cannot utilize one of these strategies, and if your retirement account does have to pay UBIT/UDFI taxes, is that the end of the world?

Not necessarily. Remember, a lot of investors who choose to self-direct their retirement accounts do so because they want to invest in something they understand and generate higher returns. The higher returns you generate can often outweigh the tax bite of these two hidden taxes.

If your IRA had $100,000 invested in mutual funds and was making an annual return of 3 percent, your IRA earned $3,000 this year. But what if your IRA instead invested that $100,000 in a fix-and-flip deal that earned a 10 percent return on investment? The IRA would have made $10,000 of income this year, and even after paying UBIT taxes of $3,700, the IRA would be left with a net profit of $6,300.

Even after paying the UBIT taxes, the IRA would still have earned more than double the return of $3,000 from mutual funds. Don't run away from an investment deal just because of the potential hidden taxes—just run the numbers before you make your investment decision!

WHAT DOES IT ALL MEAN?

Although retirement accounts grow in a tax-advantaged manner, there are two hidden tax traps that investors need to be aware of with self-directed investing. The UBIT tax can be assessed when a retirement account invests in an asset that generates ordinary income instead of investment income, which is especially tricky for investors involved in flip, wholesale, and development projects. The UDFI tax can be problematic when the retirement account invests in a property that also has debt. The taxes for both of these transactions can be very high—up to 37 percent. As with most things in the tax world, there are strategies that can help you reduce or even eliminate these hidden taxes.

Don't be quick to shy away from an investment simply because these taxes exist. Many times you may generate better returns using self-directed investing than you would in traditional investments, even after factoring in these hidden tax costs.

CHAPTER 13

USE UNCLE SAM TO HELP RAISE MONEY FOR YOUR REAL ESTATE DEALS

"Unlike sport, in business the win-win is the best possible score."

—RASHEED OGUNLARU

As real estate investors, we all know the importance of leverage. Leverage allows us to use borrowed money, purchase more investment properties, and grow our real estate at a faster pace. When talking about leverage, one of the first things that comes to mind is the traditional route of bank financing—saving up money for a down payment and then getting a loan from the bank to purchase a property. Traditional bank financing, however, comes with its own set of hurdles and restrictions, like the number of property loans that an investor may be able to obtain or the maximum loan amount that an investor can qualify for.

When it comes to raising money for your real estate deals, however, there are many different ways to invest without bank financing. In this chapter, we will focus on the tax implications of creatively financing deals and how Uncle Sam can help you raise money.

Let's be clear, we are not talking about "your" uncle "Sam." We are talking about how to use Uncle Sam, the IRS, and taxes, or rather tax savings, to help raise money for your real estate deals. Believe it or not, you may be able to use tax strategies to raise money from the property seller. Yes, you heard us right ... raising money from the seller!

Seller-Financing

Albert has had a lot of success in his first years as a real estate investor. After acquiring six rentals in his first two years, Albert decides to quit his full-time job and go all-in on his real estate strategy. His goal is to acquire five more rentals each year to build up the cash flow that he needs in order to replace his previous W-2 income.

However, one of the issues that Albert soon learns the hard way is that once he lost his W-2 income, he is no longer an attractive borrower in the eyes of a lender. In the past, he was always able to secure bank financing for his rentals without any issues. Now that he does not have any more W-2 income, it seems that none of the lenders are interested in working with him on any investment financing.

Albert recalls a creative financing strategy with which the seller would carry the note on a sold property, often referred to as "seller-financing." In this type of transaction, the property is sold to the buyer just as in a normal real estate sales transaction. The only difference is the note: In a traditional sale, the buyer obtains financing from the bank, the bank holds the note, and the buyer pays interest and principle to the bank until the note is paid in full. In the meantime, the bank holds the note as an asset, and it is secured by the underlying property. In a seller-financed deal, however, the seller is the note holder. Instead of making payments to a bank, the buyer simply makes principle and interest payments to the seller.

This creative financing structure is appealing to Albert, as he would not need to worry about obtaining bank financing and could potentially save on loan costs. In addition, he has heard that the down payment and terms of seller-financing are often a lot more flexible. From his perspective, it doesn't make a difference whether he is making payments to a bank or making payments to the seller, as long as the interest rate and loan term are both reasonable.

Albert does some research and learns that seller-financing can actually be quite attractive to the seller as well, because they can save taxes when selling a highly appreciated property. Albert decides to test the waters and makes an offer on a property that would be perfect for the BRRRR strategy. The entire inside of the house needs updates and the outside needs a face-lift.

The owner and investor, Tim, is in his eighties and is tired of managing the property himself. Tim's remaining cost basis in this property is $50,000, and the property is worth about $500,000. Between federal and state taxes, Tim's CPA has estimated taxes of close to $157,500.

Tim's Rental	
Sales Price	$500,000
Cost Basis	($50,000)
Taxable Gain	$450,000
Federal & State Tax Rates	35%
Total Taxes	$157,500

Tim's CPA had previously discussed the possibility of using a 1031 exchange to defer the taxes on the capital gains. However, that means Tim would need to reinvest $500,000 into other rentals. At this stage in his life, Tim just is not interested in selling this property simply to buy more rentals to manage. The question, though, is what would Tim do with the money if he does end up selling the property? He never felt safe investing in the stock market. In an ideal world, Tim would still like his money secured by real estate, just minus all the headaches of being a property owner.

This is the perfect opportunity: Albert is a newer investor, interested in the challenge of rehabbing a property and bringing it back up to its best use. Tim is interested in the exact opposite—he wants to get out of the landlord business as fast as he can, pay as little taxes as possible, and also keep his money secured by real estate. Both Albert and Tim should be able to achieve all their goals with seller-financing

Albert makes an offer to purchase Tim's property for $500,000. He can make a down payment of $50,000 and Tim can carry a note of $450,000. Albert can also pay Tim 6 percent interest on that note—about $27,000 annually. The note would be an interest-only note and Albert can refinance and pay off the loan in ten years. By doing this, Tim is able to defer the majority of his taxes for up to ten years.

In a seller-financed note, the seller only pays capital gains taxes on the profit portion of any gains that he receives cash for. The profit margin can be calculated by taking the total gain and dividing it by the sales price.

Profit margin = $450,000 / $500,000 = 90%

The next step is to calculate the current year taxes and gains. This is done by taking the cash received during the year for principle payments and the down payment, then multiplying that by the profit margin percentage. In Tim's example, this is an interest-only loan, so there are no principle payments beyond the $50,000 down payment.

$50,000 × 90% = $45,000

$45,000 × 35% Federal and State taxes = $15,750

Rather than paying $157,500 in taxes to the government right now, seller-financing allows Tim to sell the property and pay only $15,750 of taxes. He is able to defer $141,750 of taxes over the next ten years instead of paying it all to the IRS now. In addition, he's able to step out of his role as a landlord and continue to receive cash flow. Rather than receiving cash flow from tenants, it will be in the form of interest income from the seller-financed note. In addition, Tim's note is secured by the property, so he knows that he can foreclose on the property if Albert were to ever default on the note. Of course, Tim will still need to pay taxes on the $27,000 of interest income he earns during the year, just as if he earned interest from a bank.

In turn, the seller-financing allows Albert to purchase this rental property without bank financing. Albert is the new owner of the property and is able to receive all the tax benefits of an investor for write-offs and depreciation.

This is a win-win solution for both Albert and Tim! Here's a recap of the tax benefits from both the seller's and buyer's perspective in seller-financing

Seller-Financing	Tim (Seller)	Albert (Buyer)
Tax Deferred Capital Gains	X	
Passive Interest Income	X	
Note Secured by Real Estate	X	
Depreciation Benefit		X
Interest and Tax Deductions		X
Simpler Financing		X

In today's aging population, there are more and more property owners like Tim who are ready to step away from their properties. Some feel the need to hold on to the properties because they do not want to pay high taxes due to appreciation when they sell. Others don't know what to invest in and hesitate to put their money back into more real estate with a 1031 exchange. As an investor, make sure to highlight the potential tax benefits that may be available to the seller in a seller-financed deal. It just may be the answer that the seller has been searching for and the answer that you need, too.

Lease Option

Albert meets another property owner, Jill, who is also interested in selling her properties. Just like Tim, Jill wants to continue to receive cash flow from her properties and benefit from tax write-offs, but she simply doesn't want to continue to manage her properties. Some of the other property owners in the neighborhood started with short-term vacation rentals and were making a decent amount of cash flow. However, as a single mom with two young kids, she does not have enough time to run an Airbnb rental.

Albert has been looking for an Airbnb property, but he hasn't been able to find a property that would be a good fit. Without his W-2 job, he also can't find the necessary financing he needs.

A lease option would meet both their needs—Jill can retain her depreciation and other tax benefits and receive cash flow from the property. Albert will get access to a good short-term rental property without the need for much cash out of pocket today, and it could lock in his ability to eventually purchase the property when he can obtain the financing.

A lease option is generally composed of two contracts: a lease contract and an option to purchase contract. In a lease option, the buyer signs a lease agreement with the property owner to become a tenant. The buyer will generally pay monthly lease expenses to the property owner, just like any regular rental contract. In addition, the buyer will also sign an option-to-purchase contract, which means that the buyer will pay the seller option money immediately for the right to purchase the property at a later date in the future.

For the most part, the buyer and seller agree to a future purchase price and purchase date on the property. The buyer benefits with the ability to lock in the property at a purchase price lower than the expected future fair market value. The seller gains an interested buyer who is taking possession of the property today and is more likely to treat the property as considerately as they would treat their own real estate. The contracts generally include a stated monthly amount, options payment amount, and the future purchase amount and date. Options payments are customarily smaller than a down payment, and common lease option terms are usually from one to three years.

During the lease option period, Jill cannot sell the property to anyone else. Albert is free to use it as a short-term rental and profit on the rental arbitrage. For example, if he pays Jill $1,000 a month but collects $2,500 from his short-term rental tenants, he would get to keep the $1,500 difference ($2,500 − $1,000). If property values decline in the next few years, Albert would not be required to purchase the property. Albert may additionally have larger overall tax deductions in the short-term—100 percent of the monthly lease payments are tax-deductible in the year paid, as compared to a traditional purchase agreement where he could only deduct the mortgage interest portion of the monthly payment.

In their agreement, Albert agrees to take care of all maintenance and repairs for the property so that Jill can be hands-off. It's in Albert's best interest to keep the property in good condition because his goal is to purchase the property once he is able to obtain bank financing.

The lease would also provide Jill with some great tax savings. First, the options money she receives from Albert will not be taxed for the current year. Rather, that money becomes taxable in a few years when Albert either exercises his option or when he decides to walk away and let the option lapse. Effectively, Jill receives a lump sum of cash up front without any current taxes. If she wants, she can also receive monthly options money from Albert that would all be tax-deferred as well.

As a property owner, Jill was previously able to write off interest, taxes, repairs, and depreciation costs to reduce her total taxes. One of the greatest benefits of a lease option for Jill is that during the entire options period, she is still treated as the owner of the property. This means that she continues to take all the same tax deductions—she even retains her right to deduct depreciation on the property! If she wants to, she can use the cost segregation strategy to maximize her depreciation write-offs as well. She does not incur any capital gains taxes until Albert exercises his option to purchase the property, because even though Albert has signed an option-to-purchase contract, Jill is still treated as the owner. As a result, there are no capital gains until the property is actually sold to Albert in the future.

Here is a recap of the tax benefits from both the seller's and buyer's perspectives in using lease options.

Lease-Option	Jill (Seller)	Albert (Buyer)
Depreciation Benefit	X	
Interest and Tax Deductions	X	
Tax-Deferred Options Money	X	
Deferred Capital Gains	X	
Fully Deductible Lease Expense		X
Control of Property		X
Locked-in Purchase Price		X
Rental Income from Arbitrage		X

There is nothing to indicate that seller-financing cannot be used in conjunction with a lease option. If Albert decides to exercise his option and purchase the property from Jill after two years, Jill could offer seller-financing at that time, so Albert doesn't need to obtain financing from the bank. This way, it's easier for Albert to purchase the property and allows Jill to continue to defer any capital gains taxes, as we saw in Tim's example.

If you want to purchase a property from a flipper, a lease option may be a great negotiation tool. As discussed in Chapter 6, fix-and-flip income results in potentially high taxes. Another strategy to avoid the higher income tax is to use lease options, because they technically turn the sale of a flip into a rental.

If you're interested in a deal where the seller is a flipper, let them know that you can help them avoid high taxes by setting up a lease option instead of a straight purchase. A lease option property held for at least a year is considered an investment property. Once they hold the rental beyond 365 days, they may be able to sell it as a rental property and receive lower long-term capital gains rates.

When you eventually purchase the property, that seller may be able to conduct a 1031 like-kind exchange and defer all their taxes on this transaction. This is a powerful strategy for any real estate investor and especially powerful for those in the flipping business.

Even if their answer is no, there's no harm in asking, right?

The Important Tax Factors

There are countless creative financing techniques when it comes to real estate investing. Who gets the write-off, when you pay taxes, and what type of taxes all depend on the structure of each transaction.

In the simplest form, the "owner" of the property in question will always receive the depreciation write-off benefits. In the seller-financing example, Albert has purchased the property from Tim. Albert is the owner of the property, whereas Tim is simply the lender. As such, Albert would receive the tax benefits of depreciation. In the lease-option example with Jill, Jill is still the owner of the property, so she is eligible to take the depreciation expense. In the future, once Albert exercises his option and actually purchases the property, Albert will then be able to take the depreciation benefits.

Another important creative financing planning tip is to determine the holding period of the property. How long are you planning to hold the property? Are you planning on doing a lease option, where you lease the property for a year or two and then exercise the option to buy it and sell it sometime thereafter? Eventually, all of these questions come into play when considering which tax rate you will pay when you eventually sell the property.

Generally speaking, you want your holding period to start as soon as possible. For rental real estate, selling a property that you hold for longer than a year will typically provide the lower long-term capital gains tax treatment—which can be 15 percent, 20 percent, or even some of it tax-free at zero percent. For example, let's assume Albert purchases the property from Tim today using seller-financing, and he sells it next year for a $10,000 capital gain. He may be able to pay zero taxes on that gain if his overall tax rate remains low. Because his holding period started on the date he executed the seller-financing purchase, Albert can sell a year after taking title to the property and receive the benefit of low or no taxes on his capital gain.

Let's take the lease-option example with Jill and assume Albert executes the lease options contract today. In Year 2, he exercises the options contract and buys the property. If Albert were to sell the property in Year 2, he would not receive the lower capital gains rate because he would not have owned the property long enough. By selling before owning the property for over a year, Albert would pay taxes based on his higher ordinary tax rates. From a planning perspective, it makes a lot of sense for Albert to start the holding period sooner rather than later.

In both of these creative financing deals, Albert is able to use tax-saving strategies to help the seller reduce their tax bill, meanwhile locking up the investment properties for himself. Alongside creative real estate strategies, there are often creative tax strategies that can be deployed— the tax code is full of hidden treasures that favor the real estate investor.

Tapping Into the Retirement Gold Mine

If you are looking for more ways to use tax benefits to raise money for your real estate deals, retirement accounts are a great resource of funding to consider. Over the past decade, we have seen a significant increase in the amount of retirement funds—such as IRAs and 401(k)s—used to participate in real estate deals. In fact, research shows there are currently over $5.2 trillion[1] in retirement accounts. Imagine the deals you could do if you tapped into just a very slim portion of that to grow your real estate!

---

1 Chuck DeVore, "$5.2 Trillion of Government Pension Debt Threatens to Overwhelm State Budgets, Taxpayers," Forbes, May 31, 2019, https://www.forbes.com/sites/chuckdevore/2019/05/31/5-2-trillion-of-government-pension-debt-threatens-to-overwhelm-state-budgets-taxpayers/#42fa8ffa759d.

As a real estate investor, you will benefit from familiarizing yourself with the opportunities now available because of this trend. In the previous chapters, we discussed how to use your own retirement money for real estate investments. Well, why not teach these same strategies to others so they can do the same? When it comes to creative financing and money-raising strategies, it is crucial that you understand the impacts of retirement investing—that way, you can speak to your network of friends and family and educate them on the benefits as well.

Why should you target retirement account funds when raising money for your real estate deals, and how should this be done?

First, most people have money set aside in their retirement accounts. The majority of Americans have socked away money into traditional IRAs, Roth IRAs, 401(k)s, and pension plans, to name a few. Even though more information has come out about the benefits of self-directed investing, the vast majority of retirement accounts are still invested in traditional assets like stocks, bonds, and mutual funds. A large percentage of our population is still unaware that they can actually use their retirement money to invest in real estate.

This is where you can capture your opportunity. Next time you are meeting with some colleagues over lunch or coffee who want to get involved in real estate, why not educate them on their ability to invest in your deals using their retirement funds? If their retirement money is currently invested in the volatile stock market—or earning little to no returns in savings accounts—moving that money over to real estate can significantly increase their return on investments. If your coworker has $50,000 of Roth IRA money sitting in a certificate of deposit (CD) earning 2 percent interest, wouldn't they be better off rolling that Roth IRA money into a self-directed Roth IRA, lending it to you for your deals, and generating 4 percent or 5 percent interest instead? This can be a win-win situation in which your coworker can double their return with tax-free interest, and you can also obtain cheaper money for your next real estate deal.

If you have family or friends who have money stashed away with their current or previous employer through a 401(k) plan, they may also be able to redirect those funds into your real estate deals. Oftentimes those funds can be transferred tax- and penalty-free into a self-directed retirement account and then into your deals.

Another strategy may be to target investors who are nearing retirement age since they may soon be required by law to begin taking money out of their retirement accounts (IRAs, 401(k)s, pensions). Those amounts, which are generally invested in stocks and mutual bonds, will be taxed at the higher ordinary income rates when distributed. They can reduce taxes on their retirement distributions if they invest that money in your real estate deals after receiving the distribution from their account. If they are an equity investor in your deals, they may be able to use real estate tax benefits like write-offs, depreciation, and real estate professional status to reduce taxes from their retirement distribution income.

There are many reasons that retirement accounts are a great source of funds to use for loan investments. First, as a lender, you generate interest income. If the loan investment is made with money outside of retirement accounts, the interest income is generally taxed at your ordinary tax rate. This could be protected in a retirement account that would be either tax-deferred or tax-free.

Another reason retirement accounts are ideal for note investments is because, as a note investor, you generally have little to no expenses. You don't have repair or maintenance costs that are common for landlords. You don't currently own the real estate, so you do not have depreciation write-offs that you typically would with a rental property. An investment with little to no write-offs and no depreciation can be costly for a taxpayer. However, if you are using your retirement account for this investment, then you may not care too much about the lack of deductions since the income is already tax-deferred anyway!

Retirement money is what we consider "patient money." Unlike personal cash, it's money that has been set aside already, specifically for investment purposes. Most people are not counting on this money for their mortgage, groceries, or other monthly living expenses. This is great news for you as an investor—as long as you provide the investors with good returns, the money should remain accessible until the investor is ready to cash out at retirement age. Doesn't it sound appealing to be able to raise money once and then be able to use that money over and over in multiple deals in the future? This is why we like to refer to retirement funds as the "private money gold mine."

Before tapping into the retirement account "gold mine," you need a general understanding of how self-directed investing works. It doesn't mean you need to become a tax expert—don't feel like you need to give tax advice to your prospective investors. In fact, we highly discourage you from doing so, because you may confuse the investors more than necessary. Instead, educate your investors on their options when it comes to using retirement money in real estate. If they are interested in your deals, have them contact their CPA or tax advisor to determine how this can apply to their own unique situation.

As indicated previously, the amount of money and number of investors interested in using retirement funds for real estate investing have increased at an astounding rate in the past few years. If you want to raise some significant dollars for your next deal, make sure you get your plan in place to tap into this gold mine of an opportunity.

WHAT DOES IT ALL MEAN?

With various types of creative financing structures, there may be opportunities for tax savings. Sellers often hesitate to sell a property in fear of a potentially large tax bill. Educating them on the benefits of tax deferral with seller-financed real estate can help create a deal that may otherwise be unavailable. Seller-financing allows an investor seller to step outside of the shoes of a property owner while retaining their ability to receive monthly cash flow on a note that is secured by real estate.

For a seller who is interested in retaining the tax benefits of their rental property, a lease option may be ideal, as it allows them to continue to write off expenses for their investment property while removing them from the day-to-day management and upkeep of that property. Lease options also help the seller lock in a potential buyer and receive options money that is not taxed for several years down the road. This is also a great alternative for sellers in the fix-and-flip business who are interested in lowering their tax bill.

When looking at financing for your real estate deals, do not miss out on the opportunity to tap into the retirement accounts of other investors. If higher returns can be generated in real estate versus the stock market, it can make sense for an investor to lend their retirement money for real estate deals that can provide healthier returns with more security. Don't focus on only using your own retirement money for real estate. Speak with your friends and colleagues to see if it would make sense to supercharge their retirement assets by including them in your future deals!

CHAPTER 14
TAKING ADVANTAGE OF OPPORTUNITIES IN THE O-ZONE

"Opportunities multiply as they are seized."

—SUN TZU

The latest tax reform brought many tax-saving opportunities for the real estate industry. Tax-free income, higher deductions, lower tax rates, faster depreciation—all the changes within the latest tax reform are a windfall for a great majority of real estate investors. Another tax reform change that was implemented to encourage investor behavior is the Opportunity Zone Program. When utilized correctly, opportunity-zone investments can allow an investor to reduce, defer, and potentially eliminate taxes altogether.

The Opportunity Zone Program was created for the purpose of revitalizing certain economically distressed communities. In order to entice investors to bring money into these areas and revitalize the neighborhoods, tax breaks were provided as an incentive. The intention was to use money from private investors rather than tax dollars to improve the distressed areas—the government may have felt that investors could do a better job of improving some of these neighborhoods where the cities had been previously unsuccessful.

For many investors, putting money into distressed areas with tenants who may never pay rent may not seem an attractive investment strategy. However, the reality behind this program is very different than what you might be envisioning. The distressed areas may not be the worst neighborhoods in the city, and the tenants do not necessarily need to be those without the ability to pay rent. Before you close your mind to this possibility, you should know the three extremely useful tax benefits that the IRS is currently offering:

1. The ability to defer capital gains taxes
2. The ability to reduce a portion of the capital gains taxes
3. The ability to receive permanent tax-free gain on ten years of forced appreciation

What does all of this mean, and how does it work on paper? The best way to demonstrate the power of the Opportunity Zone Program is to walk through an example.

Benefit One: Tax Deferral

The first benefit of the Opportunity Zone Program is the ability to defer capital gains taxes in the current year. There are many different types of capital gains that may qualify for this benefit, but for illustration purposes, we will use rental real estate as an example.

Juan runs an insurance business down in Florida and owns some rentals on the side. Over the past few years, the Florida market has heated up and property prices have gone through the roof. With many baby boomers entering retirement, homes on the market are often selling for amounts far above listing prices. Juan bought a rental for $200,000 in Florida several years ago, paid down the loan over the years, and now owes around $150,000. This year, he sold the rental for $450,000, and $0 depreciation was taken—which means Juan is looking at a taxable capital gain of $250,000. Normally he would need to pay capital gains taxes of 15 percent on that gain, so the tax bill would be roughly $37,500.

Gain and Tax Calculation	
Property Sales Price	$450,000
Property Cost Basis	($200,000)
Taxable Gain	$250,000
Tax Rate	15%
Taxes Due	$37,500

Juan is nearing retirement age and he plans to spend some time traveling the world. He doesn't mind continuing to own real estate assets, but he simply wants to be a more passive investor—maybe by participating in a group investment where he can just sit back and collect cash flow without actually doing any property management.

Juan knows that he could defer his taxes with a 1031 exchange. However, that just means that he would buy a replacement rental property, which is not what he has in mind. He thought about doing a 1031 exchange and reinvesting his money into an LLC as a passive investor but found out that this was not allowed by the IRS. In addition, Juan knows that he would need to purchase a property that costs at least $450,000 if he wants to defer the taxes on all of his capital gains. If he were to take any cash out of the 1031 exchange, that cash would likely be completely taxable this year. Juan needs to find a way to sell the property, defer the taxes, reinvest in something more passive, and ideally be able to take some cash out to fund his future travel plans around the world.

The opportunity zone is a hot topic within his circle of investor friends. In fact, in his local real estate group, a few investors are involved in opportunity zone properties and had put together an opportunity zone fund. If Juan wants to defer his taxes of $37,500, one option is to invest $250,000 into the opportunity zone fund that his fellow investors put together—Florida OZone Fund, LLC.

As long as he invests $250,000 of cash into Florida OZone Fund, he would be able to defer the entire capital gains of $250,000 and save $37,500 of taxes this year. He would be able to sell his rental and pay zero upfront taxes! Plus, because he is only required to reinvest $250,000 into the opportunity zone fund, Juan would actually be able to pull out $50,000 of cash from the property sale and pay no taxes as well.

Available Cash-Out	
Sales Price	$450,000
Loan Payoff	($150,000)
Net Cash	$300,000
OZone Investment	($250,000)
Cash Out Available	$50,000

The tax deferral and cash out are both music to his ears. Juan also loves the idea of passively investing his money in an opportunity zone fund—he knows the guys managing the fund and feels that they will do a great job bringing the apartment complex to its highest and best use.

Benefit Two: Tax Reduction

The benefits do not end there. In addition to the tax deferral of $37,500, Juan also has the ability to permanently eliminate part of the capital gains taxes. This means that not only could Juan defer the $37,500 of taxes this year, he may also eliminate a portion of the taxes so that he never has to pay it in the future, either.

If Juan holds on to his investment in Florida OZone Fund, LLC, for five years, his original capital gains of $250,000 can be reduced by 10 percent down to $225,000. This means he will have a permanent tax savings on $25,000 of capital gains and never has to pay taxes on that money. In the future, Juan will only need to pay capital gains tax on $225,000.

If Juan holds his investment in Florida OZone Fund, LLC, for two additional years, he may be able to reduce his original capital gain by 15 percent. Seven years after investing in the Florida OZone Fund, LLC, his original capital gains of $250,000 would be reduced by 15 percent down to $212,500—a permanent tax savings on $37,500 of capital gains.

Benefit Three: Tax-Free Growth

Besides the current tax deferral and potential future tax reduction, Juan may receive yet another tax benefit from investing his capital gains in the Florida OZone Fund, LLC. This is the biggest potential tax benefit because it could mean 100 percent tax-free appreciation in the new opportunity zone investment property.

In our scenario, Juan invests $250,000 of his deferred capital gains into Florida OZone Fund, LLC, this year. If, during the next ten years, his share of the apartment held within the LLC appreciates from $250,000 to $375,000, then his share of the opportunity zone apartment will appreciate $125,000 in value. Because the investment in the Florida OZone Fund, LLC, was held for at least ten years, Juan could pay zero taxes on the gain that occurred on his opportunity zone property. He would *never* need to pay taxes on that $125,000 of gain.

The benefits of tax deferral, tax reduction, and tax-free growth can significantly increase the return on investment of a given deal. In our story, we deliberately oversimplified the transaction in order to demonstrate the tax-saving benefits, but as with most things in taxes, there is more to this than meets the eye. Let's go over some of the rules and potential pitfalls, and make a deeper dive into the who, what, when, and how of the Opportunity Zone Program

Who Can Invest in the Opportunity Zone?

Whether paying taxes as an individual or as an entity, all types of taxpayers are able to receive the benefits of the Opportunity Zone Program. The better question is who *should* be looking at an opportunity zone? This program was designed to help taxpayers defer capital gains taxes and have their investment grow tax-deferred and tax-free, so this can potentially be a great strategy for anyone with capital gains during the year.

However, there are many other transactions that may benefit. In the past, nothing in the tax law existed that could help a stock investor defer taxes on their capital gains. Let's say you invested in a start-up company that did extremely well, and within a few months, your investment had increased $50,000 in value. If you felt it was time to cash out of that stock and reinvest that money elsewhere, you would need to pay capital gains taxes on that profit. Assuming a short-term capital gains tax rate of 40 percent between federal and state taxes, you would need to pay the government $20,000. This would leave you with only $30,000 to reinvest.

One of the surprising benefits of the Opportunity Zone Program is that it also applies to capital gains from stock sales. If you wanted to, you could defer the $20,000 of taxes by reinvesting the entire $50,000 gain into an opportunity zone fund. Not only that, but you could get access to the original cash you used to purchase the stock (that is, your stock basis) without any current taxes due. Just as in Juan's example, if you hold that fund investment for more than five or seven years, part of your deferred taxes of $20,000 goes away. If you hold the investment for more than ten years, the entire appreciation related to your investment in the asset may be tax-free forever. If you are looking to sell highly appreciated stock holdings and redirect that money into real estate, the opportunity zone fund can be a powerful strategy.

On a similar note, opportunity zone benefits also may be applicable to someone selling their business. If you have built a business—or have invested in someone else's business—and would like to shift that asset into real estate, any capital gains from the sale of your business interest may also receive the opportunity zone tax benefits.

Essentially, the Opportunity Zone Program can defer and reduce all sorts of capital gains taxes—whether they're from the sale of real estate, stocks, business interests, or even cryptocurrency. And the opportunity zone may be beneficial for homeowners; if a married couple were to sell their primary home for a gain of $600,000, generally only the first $500,000 could be tax-free if they meet the residency requirements of the primary home tax gain exclusion. They could, however, invest that $100,000 into an opportunity zone fund to receive the tax benefits. Even if this couple did not meet the primary home tax gain exclusion, they could reinvest the entire $600,000 of capital gains in the opportunity zone, even though they never turned their primary home into a rental.

As you can see, the Opportunity Zone Program can help provide tax benefits to all types of taxpayers with capital gains income. Besides the tax-deferral and reduction, many are looking down the road to the tax-free gain of the investment once the ten-year holding period is over. In special circumstances, it may even benefit an investor to strategically create a capital gains situation so they can utilize the gain and invest into an opportunity zone.

What Is an Opportunity Zone Property?

An opportunity zone is an economically distressed community that has been approved by the Secretary of the U.S. Treasury where the government wants to see improvement. Often when you hear the words *opportunity zone property*, images of abandoned buildings or run-down shopping centers with graffiti may pop up in your mind. For this reason, many investors shy away from looking into opportunity zone investments.

This isn't necessarily the case. If you pull up the designated opportunity zone area maps from the government website, you will see that these designated areas exist all across the nation. From states like Colorado and Minnesota to coastal locations in California and Florida, opportunity zone areas exist even in some of the country's most desirable locations. You may be surprised to learn that there are actually opportunity zone areas in highly sought-after markets like the wine country in Santa Barbara and various islands in Hawaii.

Unfortunately, simply buying a property that is listed on the IRS opportunity zone website will not automatically qualify you for these wonderful tax benefits. Because the government's goal is to improve these distressed communities, the tax code does have some additional requirements that must be met in order for a property to fall within the definition of an opportunity zone property. It must meet all of these four requirements:

First, the property must be located within the government designated opportunity zone areas. The opportunity zone benefits, however, are not only limited to the property itself. If you don't want direct ownership of a property, you can also purchase partnership interest, stock, or business interest that holds the asset that is located within the opportunity zone.

The second requirement is simple: the property must be purchased after December 31, 2017. For leased properties, you must enter into the lease agreement after December 31, 2017.

The third requirement is that the investor needs to make substantial improvements to the purchased property within a thirty-month period. Of course, there are countless ways to improve a property. In real estate terms, this means that the owner must invest an amount that's at least equal to the purchase price of the building. If you purchased an opportunity zone duplex for $200,000—and $50,000 of the purchase price was allocated to land and $150,000 was allocated to the building—you would need to put in at least $150,000 of improvements into this property. These improvements need to be done within a thirty-month period, and practically speaking, this may be one of the more difficult requirements to meet. If you don't want to invest a large amount of time and effort into a property's improvement, this hurdle could be hard to overcome.

Take note that there are a few exceptions to this rule. Substantial improvements are not required if you invest in raw land, leased properties, or newly constructed properties in the opportunity zone. If your investment is in a building that has been abandoned for more than five years, then it can also avoid the substantial improvements test—the IRS assumes you will already be doing a lot of work to an abandoned property, so they do not assign a dollar amount to the necessary improvements.

The fourth and final requirement is that, in order to be eligible as an opportunity zone property, the property must be held by an opportunity zone fund.

What Is an Opportunity Zone Fund?

An opportunity zone fund is an investment vehicle set up as a legal entity. The fund must be a legal entity within the United States that files its own tax returns, like S corporations, C corporations, partnerships, or multi-member LLCs. This means that you wouldn't be able to simply purchase a property in your personal name or in a single member LLC. The legal documents of the entity must also include a statement indicating its purpose to invest in a qualified opportunity zone property and indicating the entity's plans to adhere to the tax and regulatory requirements.

The opportunity zone fund must also hold at least 90 percent of its assets in qualified opportunity zone properties. For example, if you have an entity that holds a $50,000 property in an opportunity zone and also holds $150,000 of real estate that is outside of the opportunity zone, the entity could not be considered an opportunity zone fund. Therefore, there would be no tax benefits for this opportunity zone property, even if you meet all the other requirements of the IRS. As such, we highly recommend using a new entity to act as an opportunity zone fund to hold only opportunity zone properties, not an existing entity that holds other non-opportunity zone properties.

Last but not least, a self-certification must be made by the fund each year by filing Form 8996 with its federal income tax return by the return's due date with the IRS. This rule is extremely important because if the opportunity zone fund's entity tax return is filed late, it would not receive the related tax benefits.

When Are the Deadlines for Opportunity Zone Investments?

As with many things in taxes, there are strict timelines in order to receive the opportunity zone tax benefits. The first timeline applies to the taxpayer, who has 180 days from the date the capital gains occurred to reinvest that money into an opportunity zone fund. Once those 180 days have passed, that gain is no longer eligible for the opportunity zone tax benefits.

There is, however, a loophole for investors who invest through a legal entity. For example, Grace was one of thirty passive investors who own an apartment building through Longhorn, LLC. When the LLC sells the apartment building on February 1—because Grace's interest in the apartment was through the LLC—the gain is instead treated as if it occurred on December 31 of that year. For Grace, this means the 180-day clock to then reinvest her capital gains into an opportunity zone fund starts on December 31 of that year instead of February 1.

The second timeline applies to the opportunity zone fund itself. Let's continue with our example: Grace decides to reinvest her money into Kansas OZone Fund, LLC, which plans to raise money from investors and use that to invest in an apartment within the opportunity zone coordinates. Kansas OZone Fund, LLC, has 180 days to purchase the Kansas apartment building. In summary, Grace has 180 days to reinvest her capital gains in opportunity zone funds, and the Fund itself has 180 days to purchase the property.

The Ugly Side of the Opportunity Zone Program

As with everything in taxes, you have to take the bad with the good, and this tax break is no exception. A big pitfall of the opportunity zone is the requirement to pay taxes by the property sale date or December 31, 2026, whichever is earlier. This means that the investor can only defer the original capital gains taxes until 2026, regardless of whether they sell the investment or if they decide to continue holding on to the property. The key is to make sure you have liquidity available to you when you need to pay the taxes!

Putting It All Together

For a better understanding of opportunity zones, let's go over a comprehensive example on how this could work. Keep in mind that the example below has been drastically simplified to make it easier to follow.

Bob has owned an apartment in Nevada for over ten years. This year, he sold the apartment and had taxable capital gains of $1,500,000, and instead of paying $300,000 of capital gains taxes, Bob decides to reinvest all his capital gains into a Florida OZone Fund. Bob pays no capital gains taxes this year on the sale of his Nevada apartment.

After holding this investment in Florida OZone Fund, LLC, for seven years, Bob's capital gains are permanently reduced by 15 percent, down to $1,275,000. At a 20 percent capital gains tax rate, Bob saved $45,000 in taxes. However, in 2026, Bob is required to pay taxes on the remainder of his deferred capital gains from the sale of his Nevada apartment of $1,275,000.

Nevada Apartment	
Gain on Sale	$1,500,000
15% Reduction of Gain after 7 Years	**($225,000)**
Adjusted Tax Deferred Gain	$1,275,000
Capital Gains Tax Rate	20%
Taxes Due in Year 2026	$255,000

Bob decides to continue holding on to the property, and after ten years of ownership, Bob would also be able to receive permanent tax-free appreciation on the apartment held in Florida OZone Fund, LLC. At the end of ten years, the Florida apartment is now worth $2,700,000. Assuming a simple $0 for depreciation, here is what the benefit looks like:

Florida Apartment	
Fair Market Value after 10 Years	$2,700,000
Tax Basis after 2026 Gain Recognition	($1,500,000)
Tax-Free Gain	$1,200,000
Capital Gains Tax Rate	20%
Total Permanent Tax Savings	$240,000

In this example, Bob would be able to pay zero taxes on the appreciation of his Florida apartment and save up to $240,000 of taxes permanently. This is a tax windfall with which he receives all three benefits: tax deferral, tax reduction, and tax-free growth.

Opportunity Zone Versus 1031 Exchange

Does the Opportunity Zone Program remind you of another strategy that we discussed previously in this book? If you're thinking of the 1031 exchange tax-deferral strategy, you are not alone! The Opportunity Zone Program does have some similarities to the 1031 exchange. They both have a reinvestment time frame of 180 days, and both strategies are designed to help you defer capital gains taxes today. There are, however, some major differences between the two strategies.

One of the major benefits of the 1031 exchange that is not available to the Opportunity Zone Program is that the 1031 exchange allows you to potentially defer taxes indefinitely. If you wanted to, you could use 1031 exchanges to sell one property, replace it with another property, then sell the second property and replace it with the third property, and so on. There are no restrictions to how many 1031 exchanges you can perform as a real estate investor. In fact, one of the greatest strategies is the ability to use 1031 exchanges until the properties may be passed to your beneficiaries with little to no capital gains taxes. The opportunity zone, on the other hand, only helps you defer your original capital gains taxes until the year 2026. Again, this means that you would need to pay taxes on the deferred gain in 2026 regardless of whether or not you sell the property.

Having said that, there are many benefits of the Opportunity Zone Program that you may not receive with a 1031 exchange. In fact, an opportunity zone investment can be a great last-minute strategy for investors who either failed a 1031 exchange or have taxable money from a 1031 exchange transaction that they would like to defer taxes on.

The chart below highlights some of the many benefits:

Opportunity Zone Program	1031 Exchange
You only need to reinvest the capital gains portion into the opportunity zone fund in order to defer taxes (for example, you can sell your property, take some cash out, reinvest the remaining cash, and still defer 100 percent of your taxes)	You generally must reinvest the entire sales proceeds in order to defer taxes
Eligible for a permanent tax reduction if held longer than 5 years	Capital gains in a 1031 exchange are only deferred and not reduced
May be eligible for tax-free appreciation if the asset is held over 10 years	No tax-free appreciation using the 1031 exchange strategy, unless it is passed on to the next generation upon death
May be more flexible; no 45-day identification rule	45-day identification rule must be met
Intermediary not required	Intermediary required

Opportunity or Trap

Although the Opportunity Zone Program provides some extremely powerful tax-saving benefits, many hurdles and requirements must be met in order to qualify. If you are not a highly experienced investor with large improvement projects, you may be better off considering investing passively. Rather than doing these large improvement projects on your own, there are many syndications with which you can be a private equity investor in opportunity zone funds. The upside of being a passive investor in a larger deal is that you may be able to receive these tax benefits without needing to do all the work.

With the substantial tax benefits of the Opportunity Zone Program, it could be easy for anyone to get overly excited and forget to analyze an opportunity on its own merits. When considering investments in qualified opportunity zone funds, don't forget the fundamentals. Scrutinize the deals and do your due diligence just as you would with any other investment decisions.

In other words, don't let the tax tail wag the investment dog. As with any investment, it is extremely important to evaluate the non-tax benefits of the deal. The tax benefits are useless if the qualified opportunity zone fund fails. Alternatively, a well-performing investment can be a great windfall from both an investment and tax perspective.

WHAT DOES IT ALL MEAN?

The benefits of the Opportunity Zone Program include current tax deferral, potential future tax reduction, and potential tax-free growth. By offering this benefit, the government intends to incentivize investors to improve specific neighborhoods and bring business and income into these areas. Although some eligible properties exist in distressed neighborhoods, many investors are pleasantly surprised to find opportunity zone properties located in some of America's nicer neighborhoods, as well.

To be eligible for the tax benefits of the Opportunity Zone Program, the investment must be made in an opportunity zone fund within 180 days from the sale of the capital gains asset. This opportunity zone fund must hold the property that is located within the government designated opportunity zones, and the investor must also make substantial improvements to the property. Outside of rental real estate, other capital gains transactions such as stock sales, business sales, and even primary residence sales may also be eligible for the tax benefits of the Opportunity Zone Program.

One major downside of the program is that the deferred capital gain becomes taxable in the year 2026 regardless of whether the opportunity zone asset is sold or not. Even given all of the potential tax benefits of opportunity zone investments, don't lose sight of your investment criteria and make sure to perform the usual analysis and due diligence before making your final investment decision.

CHAPTER 15
THE PERFECT TAX PLAN

"A goal without a plan is just a wish."

—ANTOINE DE SAINT-EXUPÉRY

In the beginning of this book we talked about how Amazon, the world's largest retailer, was able to pay zero corporate taxes in a year when it made $9.4 billion in net profits. The company was able to utilize many of the government-provided tax breaks to wipe out its entire tax liability. There wasn't one save-all strategy; rather, the company used a combination of strategies to achieve the desired tax-free year.

By cracking the tax code, we saw in this book how tax strategies that are specifically designed to benefit real estate investors can reduce the amount of money they lose to taxes each and every year. Although not all the strategies discussed in this book will apply to your own unique situation, those that are applicable can save you thousands of dollars in taxes if implemented correctly. Even better, the tax strategies you learned in this book do not need to work in isolation. In fact, several tax strategies can often be utilized together in the same year, and the tax-saving results can be astonishing.

The Power of Proactive Tax Planning

Nathan and Lori had been working with the same tax preparer—a close family friend who had also helped file taxes for Nathan's parents and siblings—for as long as they could remember. However, they noticed that every year as their income increased, so did their tax bill. Every year they would complain to their tax person that their taxes went up, and every year they were told, "When you make more money, you pay more taxes!"

Nathan and Lori were losing close to 50 percent of their income to taxes every year, and they knew there had to be a better way to manage their tax bill. That was when they first came to us for proactive tax planning. Because they were making more money than before, Nathan and Lori knew that it was going to be a high tax year again and wanted to make sure they put a plan in place to legally reduce their tax bill.

Nathan had a successful online business selling cell phone accessories, while Lori managed their rental portfolio. The income from Nathan's online business was steadily increasing, and the past year had been his best—his business made just over $360,000 in net profits.

Nathan and Lori owned a handful of rental properties that brought them $2,000 of cash flow every month, so that year they profited about $24,000. One of their rentals was a duplex that they had purchased many years ago; it had appreciated about $40,000, but the cash flow on the property was not great. With all the recent opportunities in the short-term rental market, Lori was considering selling the duplex and using the money to purchase a lakefront condo that she could rent out as a short-term vacation rental. Nathan and Lori also wanted to rent out their primary home on Airbnb while they traveled on a monthlong trip to Europe. Due to the peak summer season demand, they would be able to rent out their home for fourteen days and make a profit of $8,400.

Here is a summary of the various income items that Nathan and Lori were expecting for the year:

Nathan's Online Income	$360,000
Rental Income	$24,000
Gain On Sale of Rental	$40,000
Rental Income from Primary Home	$8,400
Total Income	$432,400

Now the fun part: Let's take a look at some of the strategies that we identified during the tax-planning process to help Nathan and Lori reduce their tax bill.

Let's start with the easy one. If you will recall from Chapter 5, renting out your home for fourteen days or less results in completely tax-free rental income. Since Nathan and Lori did not rent out their home for more than fourteen days, the entire $8,400 while traveling for vacation was completely tax-free. Not a bad way to make some tax-free money while you are away, right?

Now let's move on to other strategies to reduce Nathan and Lori's tax bill. First and foremost, we needed to find ways to reduce taxes for Nathan's consulting income. Consulting income is the highest taxed income because it's subject to federal and state income taxes *and* self-employment taxes. While reviewing their previous years' tax returns, we noticed that Nathan had missed out on many of the legitimate deductions he could have claimed for his business. Although Nathan worked from home for his online business, he never claimed a home office deduction. The reason? Because his tax preparer had told him it was a big audit risk. After Nathan realized that this was just a myth, we worked with him to calculate his home office write-off at about $12,000 for the year.

We also noticed that Nathan was not taking any car-related expenses. Although his business was selling cell phone accessories online, there were plenty of instances where Nathan had to drive to the local office supply store, to the post office, or to meet with vendors, so there were plenty of tax-deductible car costs that he was missing out on. Similarly, Nathan learned that he could write off other expenses such as business meals, the business use portion for his own cell phone, and other office items.

Now that their daughter had graduated from college, she was interested in helping out with the online sales and making some money on the side. We worked with Nathan to hire her in the business and legally shift income from his higher tax bracket into her lower tax bracket. These strategies combined generated enough expenses to reduce his taxable consulting income from $360,000 down to $330,000.

Nathan and Lori had not done much to save toward retirement, and now that they were making more income, they wanted to set some money aside to take advantage of the tax-deferred growth. We worked with them to put together a Solo 401(k) and defined benefit plan combo, and they were able to contribute about $200,000 to reduce their taxes. Because

Nathan and Lori wanted to continue investing in real estate, we recommended they set up the retirement accounts with self-directed custodians so they could have better control of that money.

Once the money was in the retirement account, Nathan immediately started shopping for investments and purchased two smaller rentals in his self-directed retirement account. Between the newfound business deductions and retirement planning strategies, Nathan's income was now reduced from $360,000 to $130,000.

Nathan's online income: $360,000

Business deductions: −$30,000

Retirement contributions: −$200,000

New taxable income: $130,000

As part of the proactive tax planning process, we found out that Lori was planning to sell their duplex for a large gain. Because she planned to reinvest her money in the lakefront condo, we knew that a 1031 exchange would apply perfectly. It would allow her to take her profit from the duplex and buy the new lakefront rental without owing anything to the IRS until later. Since Lori had followed all of the 1031 exchange rules, she would pay no taxes that year on the $40,000 gain from the duplex sale.

Although Lori had managed their own rentals for several years, she never claimed to be a real estate professional on their tax return. As a result, she was never able to use her rental losses to offset Nathan's income from his online business. Her old tax preparer used to tell her that because she was not a licensed Realtor, she would not be able to use the tax benefits. However, during the proactive tax-planning process, we worked with Lori to understand which tasks she performed for her rental properties. Because she spent over 750 hours in her rental properties, she would qualify as a real estate professional, so she could start to use rental losses to offset the taxes from Nathan's online income.

One way to supercharge that tax strategy is to accelerate the depreciation on all of their rental properties using cost segregation. When we reviewed their old tax returns, we noticed that they had been depreciating their rentals using the slowest method allowed by the IRS. Now that

Lori would qualify as a real estate professional, it was the best time to do a cost segregation—we were able to recalculate depreciation using faster time frames to create a very large up-front tax deduction, rather than waiting many years to receive that tax benefit. The total accelerated depreciation was $65,000 for all their rental properties—not only did that wipe out the taxes from their $24,000 of rental income, but the remaining $41,000 loss was able to offset taxes for Nathan's online income as well!

As a final comparison, let's take a look at Nathan and Lori's taxes with and without proactive tax planning:

	Without Tax Planning	With Tax Planning
Nathan's Online Income	$360,000	$130,000
Rental Income/(Loss)	$24,000	($41,000)
Gain on Sale of Rental	$40,000	—
Rental Income from Primary Home	$8,400	
Total Income	$432,400	$89,000
Fed/State Tax Rate	44%	28%
Total Taxes	$190,256	$24,920
Total Taxes Saved		**$165,336**

With proactive tax planning, Nathan and Lori were able to lower their tax bill by more than $165,000 in just one year. Imagine how much they had probably been overpaying in previous years! When we first met Nathan and Lori, they were simply hoping to cut down on their taxes. They never imagined that the results would be this significant—in addition to saving $165,000 in taxes, they also now had $200,000 growing tax-advantaged in their retirement account. The results of the proactive tax planning really opened their eyes to how tax law could be used to their advantage. They can now take full control of their finances and supercharge their path toward financial freedom.

Take Action on Taxes
Take a look at successful investors. One of the main underlying charac-

teristics that you will see among them is their ability to *take action*. It's one thing to learn about tax and investing strategies, and it is another thing to actually put those ideas to work. Without changing your underlying facts, it may be impossible to change your tax situation.

We are not saying you should run out now and form a legal entity for your real estate. Nor are we saying you definitely need to hire someone for accelerated depreciation. Creating massive tax deductions and controlling your taxes is not something that can be done overnight, and it is also not something that can be done in a brief thirty-minute meeting with your tax advisor. True tax savings are only achieved with proactive tax planning. As mentioned previously, tax planning is a process that takes time, analysis, and careful consideration.

If you have spent countless hours online reading tax strategies for real estate investors, it also does not necessarily mean you have sufficient understanding to implement a particular strategy. Time and time again, we meet investors who fall victim to poorly implemented strategies. Sometimes they jump the gun and implement something without good professional guidance, or sometimes they work with an advisor who is not well versed in real estate—and these mistakes may be extremely costly.

As you have seen through the many examples in this book, there are major differences in tax results, even when the smallest detail is missed. For example, when implemented correctly, a 1031 exchange can help defer taxes forever—but missing the deadlines of a 1031 exchange can cause your entire transaction to come crumbling down. Qualifying as a real estate professional can help wipe out your entire tax bill for the year—but not legitimately meeting real estate professional status can result in zero tax savings for the year and cost you more in taxes in future years. Following the rules when using retirement funds for your real estate deals can super-charge your assets for future retirement—but using retirement money incorrectly can result in large taxes and expensive penalties.

As the saying goes, the devil is in the details. This is why it is extremely important to consult with your tax advisor before implementing any strategies that you may hear or read about. Because everyone's situation is different and unique, a strategy that works for your neighbor or for your friend from the local real estate investment club may or may not work the same for you.

Whom Can You Count On?

The concepts we discussed can be extremely complex, so you wouldn't want to execute them without professional guidance. If your sister is currently in college and has taken some accounting courses, she still may not be a tax expert. She might not be the best person to pull the trigger on some of the strategies you learned in this book.

Believe it or not, all tax advisors are not created equally. There is a distinct difference between tax return preparers and tax advisors. Tax return preparers are reactive—they review the information on your activities last year and report those on the appropriate forms. Tax advisors think proactively—they work with you throughout the year to look ahead at future transactions, and they provide options for certain decisions that can produce better tax results.

Unfortunately, many CPAs are busy day in and day out with filing tax returns and responding to IRS notices. Even for the most well-intentioned tax professionals, there often isn't enough time to keep up-to-date on all the tax changes that occur throughout the year and to research the latest strategies.

So how do you know if you are working with the right tax advisor?

The right tax advisor is actually not hard to identify. It has nothing to do with how many years someone has practiced doing taxes—we have met many tax preparers who have been in the industry for decades, but they still don't have a good grasp of the tax loopholes for real estate investors. A good tax advisor may not have graduated from one of the top universities or accounting programs. In fact, very few of the strategies discussed in this book are taught in college. The right tax advisor may or may not hold the highest designations—just because someone is a Certified Public Accountant (CPA), it does not mean they are well versed in real estate tax strategies. We have met and worked with many great tax advisors who hold lesser designations who have been able to refine their skills by specializing in a specific niche like real estate.

Whether or not the person is the right tax advisor for you actually has more to do with their entire approach. Are they proactive or reactive? One big indicator of a good tax advisor is that they ask *you* the questions. Does your tax advisor ask you questions, or are they in a hurry to move on to the next client? If you're working with the right person, they should be working for *you* and not for the IRS.

The dialogue between you and your tax advisor should also be very candid and open. They should be someone you are extremely comfortable in speaking with. Make sure you tell them about all your transactions so they can give you the most appropriate advice. If you feel the need to withhold information from your tax advisor, that could mean you are in the wrong relationship. We often tell our clients to inform us of everything that occurs in their life—beyond real estate, some other important items to discuss with your tax advisor can range from major life events such as marriage, divorce, relocation, job changes, kids, and minor occurrences like throwing a party or planning a vacation trip. These are all opportunities for potential tax savings from a tax-planning perspective. Your main role in working proactively with your tax advisor is to inform them of your transactions before they take place. This way, they can advise you to take advantage of any tax-saving opportunities.

An important thing to understand is that, contrary to popular belief, April is not the time to ask your CPA a lot of questions on how to reduce your taxes on last year's income. Ask those questions much earlier! It is extremely important for your tax advisor to take the time to get to know you—and we don't just mean "get to know you" in terms of what you did last year to be able to fill out the tax return. Getting to know you means getting to know your plans, your hopes, and your dreams. Yes, we understand that sounds more like a personal therapy session. The truth is, when we do tax planning, oftentimes it does feel a little bit like a therapy session.

With proactive tax planning, a good tax advisor should be asking you personal questions. Why? Because your tax advisor needs to know your entire profile before providing any relevant and impactful answers, and that is not just restricted to taxes and real estate. For example, one of the first questions we always ask is "What are your short-term and long-term goals?" Another one might be "Where do you see yourself in the next three to five years?" Yes, we understand these are not questions you expect to hear from your tax advisors. For some, they may be difficult questions to answer, but they are important because your answers to these questions can change the way your tax strategies are shaped.

For example, if you indicated that in the next three to five years you plan to have kids and stop working full-time, real estate professional status may be a great strategy to work toward. You may be planning on investing in real estate, as well as opening up a new business that is not real estate–related. Depending on the type and the amount of income you might be earning from that business, it may be beneficial to look at different types of entity structuring to reduce taxes on that income. What if you wanted to help take care of other family members financially? In that case, income shifting may be a good strategy—such as hiring your family members to work in your real estate business, and then you can take a legitimate deduction for the money that you are paying them. Strategies like this can be an extremely powerful tax-saving technique because they help you take a tax deduction for things you are already spending money on.

Not all investors are landlords. If you are interested in fix-and-flip, we may want to look at strategies to minimize the high taxes and consider other strategies—such as tax deferral and expense maximization—to offset that income. You might want to grow your real estate brokerage business. In that scenario, maybe the appropriate entity structure and ideal retirement account are important strategies.

Another surprising question we often ask our tax-planning clients is "What are any causes that you are passionate about?" With the appropriate charitable tax planning, you can help the charities you would like to support by using donations to save taxes, meanwhile keeping the asset for you and your beneficiaries in the future.

Tax Planning by Design

Successful real estate investments happen by design and not by chance. You don't just randomly purchase a property and expect to automatically receive great cash flow and appreciation. Careful consideration and analysis are generally done on the marketplace, tenants, rents, expected future appreciation potential, and eventual exit strategy.

The same goes for taxes—as taxpayers, we cannot simply do nothing and expect to receive great tax savings just because we are real estate investors. Tax planning happens by design. It requires a proactive and holistic look at your entire financial and personal profile. It involves careful scrutiny—along with properly implemented steps—to ensure that the optimal tax savings goal is received.

Many tax strategies discussed in this book can be utilized year after year. Understanding the tax loopholes, and using them correctly to control your tax bill, means keeping more of your hard-earned money. This means more money to invest and more money to grow your wealth.

Oftentimes the money that you save from taxes can be the easiest money you will ever make.

As demonstrated by the stories in this book, tax strategies can work together synergistically to create some powerful results. Various strategies can fit together perfectly like pieces of a puzzle—once that puzzle is complete, you can see your own tax savings from utilizing these strategies. Then you will know that you, too, have taken control of your taxes. Congratulations on cracking the tax code!

APPENDIX A

In order for an investor to take advantage of the safe harbor rules to claim rental income as eligible for the pass-through tax benefit, a signed statement must be attached to the filing copy of the tax return. The statement must be signed and dated by the taxpayer under penalties of perjury. Here is a sample of the safe harbor statement for rental investors.

IRC §199A RENTAL REAL ESTATE SAFE HARBOR STATEMENT

Taxpayer: John Smith
Taxpayer SSN/EIN: 111-22-3333
Tax Year: 20XX
Property or properties making up real estate enterprise:

Property address	Type of property (residential / commercial)
123 Main Street Los Angeles, CA 90210	Residential
321 Frontier Street Memphis, TN 23055	Residential
1100 Cain Circle Miami, FL 65233	Residential

This statement confirms that all requirements for the safe harbor pursuant to IRS Notice 2019-07 have been satisfied to claim this rental real estate enterprise for the qualified business income (QBI) deduction.

Specifically, I (we) affirm all of the following:

- Separate books and records are maintained to reflect income and expenses for this real estate enterprise;
- 250 or more hours of services were performed with respect to this real estate enterprise for the tax year;
- No part of the real estate enterprise was used as a residence for any part of the year; and
- No part of the real estate enterprise was rented or leased under a triple net lease.

Under penalties of perjury, I (we) declare that I (we) have examined the statement, and, to the best of my (our) knowledge and belief, the statement contains all the relevant facts relating to the revenue procedure, and such facts are true, correct, and complete.

_____

Signed (Taxpayer)   Date

_____

Printed name   Title

_____

Signed (Taxpayer)   Date

_____

Printed name   Title

APPENDIX B

One of the requirements for receiving the tax benefits of being a real estate professional is the material participation test. The IRS has defined material participation to reflect situations where the investor is able to show they are working on their rental properties in a regular, continuous, and substantial manner. In order to determine whether investors qualify for material participation, the IRS has provided seven tests. Remember, the taxpayer does not need to meet all seven tests. As long as the investor can meet one of the tests below, the material participation requirement can be met.

SEVEN TESTS FOR MATERIAL PARTICIPATION

To qualify for material participation for a tax year, the investor only needs to answer yes to one of the following questions:
- Did you work more than 500 hours in the rental activity during the year?
- Did you perform substantially all of the work in this activity, as compared to everyone else who worked in this activity during the year (including non-owners)?
- Did you spend at least 100 hours in the rental activity and spend more time than any other individual?
- If you spent at least 100 hours during the year on each of your rental activities, but you can't pass any of the other material participation tests listed herein, then you can still qualify for material participation if your total hours combined for all of your rentals exceeds 500 for the year.
- Did you meet the material participation test at least five out of the last ten years?

- If this is a personal service activity, did you meet the material participation requirement for any of the three prior years?
- Under all the facts and circumstances, did you participate in the activity on a regular, continuous, and substantial basis during the year?

Spouse's Time: For purposes of the seven material participation tests above, your time spent in an activity includes your spouse's participation time as well. This applies even if you do not file a joint return with your spouse and/or even if your spouse doesn't own an interest in the activity.

APPENDIX C

As mentioned in Appendix B, one requirement for receiving the tax benefits of being a real estate professional is that an investor must pass one of the material participation tests. The investor can make an election to combine all of their rental activities together as one activity in order to meet the time requirements test. This means that instead of spending 500 hours on every single rental property, the investor instead combines the properties and meets the requirement, as long as they spend at least 500 hours on all of their rentals combined. Here is a sample of the election to combine rental activities as a single activity.

This statement does not need to be signed but does need to be attached to the filing copy of the tax return that is submitted to the IRS.

ELECTION TO COMBINE RENTAL REAL ESTATE INTERESTS INTO ONE ACTIVITY PURSUANT TO CODE

SEC. 469(C)(7)(A) AND REG. §1.469-9

John and Jane Smith
123 Main St.
Anywhere USA, CA 12345

Identification Number: 123-45-6789

Tax Year End: 12/31/20XX

The taxpayer hereby elects to combine all rental real estate interests into one activity pursuant to Code Sec. 469(c)(7)(A) and Reg. §1.469-9. The taxpayer elects to treat all of the taxpayer's interests in rental real estate as a single rental real estate activity for this tax year and subsequent tax years. The taxpayer declares itself a "qualifying taxpayer," as defined by Code Sec. 469(c)(7)(B).

APPENDIX D

When you have a property that is used as both a rental property and personal property, the tax treatment can be different, depending on the profile of the property. Use the flowchart below to help you navigate the differences in the various tax treatments.

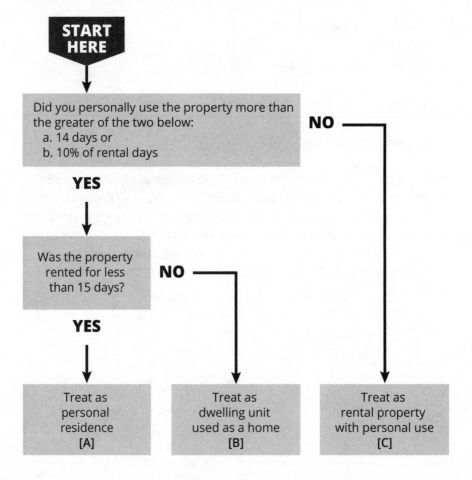

[A] When your property is treated as a personal residence, all the rental income for this property is tax-free. In addition, you can still deduct 100 percent of the mortgage interest and property taxes on your primary home as usual. Keep in mind, though, that because the rental income is tax-free, there is also no deduction for any rental-related expenses.

[B] When your property is treated as a dwelling unit used as a second home, the rental income earned from the property is taxable. As a result, the rental-related expenses are deductible against this rental income. You would prorate the expenses of this property between rental and personal use for the year. Certain rental-related expenses for this property may be limited to the income generated from this property.

[C] When your property is treated as a rental property with personal use, this means that all of the income from this rental property is taxable. All rental-specific expenses are deductible and the prorated rental expenses of the home can also be deductible. Prorated personal use property taxes can be deductible, although prorated personal use mortgage interest is non-deductible.

ACKNOWLEDGEMENTS

We would like to express our deepest gratitude to the many people who made this book possible.

First and foremost is the wonderful family that surrounds us. Thank you to our amazing parents and grandparents who have supported and inspired us to reach for the stars. To our extended family and friends, thank you for the love you have provided during every step of our journey. To our amazing son Austin: you have shown us a love we never knew was possible. And to our baby boy Mason, seven years later: you completed our family circle, and every day is more fun than the day before.

Thank you to all of our team members at Keystone CPA, Inc. who helped us to develop the strategies in this book. Your daily commitment to servicing the firm and its clients with dedication and passion has made this book possible. It's been a fun journey. A special thank you to Upnik Patel and Mina Foisia, who went the extra mile to help us put this book together.

Thank you to our colleagues and mentors over the years for challenging us to be the best advisors that we can be. Your experience, knowledge, and guidance have enabled us to build a firm that we are very proud of.

Thank you, as well, to the thousands of clients over the years that have put your trust in us. You have taught us at least as much as we taught you, and this book would not have been possible without your input and ideas.

Finally, a special thank you to Josh Dorkin, Brandon Turner, Scott Trench, Katie Miller, Kaylee Pratt, the editors and designers of this book, and the entire community at BiggerPockets.com. Your hard work at BiggerPockets has allowed us to once again share our passion on tax-saving strategies with real estate investors everywhere.

It takes a village, and we are grateful for ours. To all of these people, thank you!

More from BiggerPockets Publishing

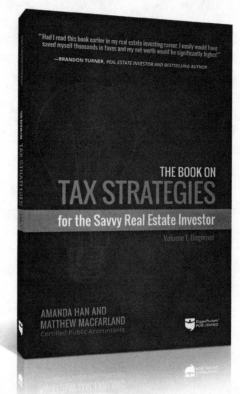

The Book on Tax Strategies for the Savvy Real Estate Investor, Volume 1

Taxes! Boring and irritating, right? Perhaps. But if you want to succeed in real estate, your tax strategy will play a huge role in how fast you grow. A great tax strategy can save you thousands of dollars a year. A bad strategy could land you in legal trouble. From Amanda Han and Matthew MacFarland's *The Book on Tax Strategies for the Savvy Real Estate Investor*, you will find ways to deduct more, invest smarter, and pay far less to the IRS!

If you enjoyed this book, we hope you'll take a moment to check out some of the other great material BiggerPockets offers. BiggerPockets is the real estate investing social network, marketplace, and information hub, designed to help make you a smarter real estate investor through podcasts, books, blog posts, videos, forums, and more. Sign up today—it's free! **Visit www.BiggerPockets.com.**

Buy, Rehab, Rent, Refinance, Repeat

Invest in real estate and never run out of money . . . using the hottest strategy in the real estate world! In *Buy, Rehab, Rent, Refinance, Repeat,* you'll discover the incredible strategy known as BRRRR—a long-hidden secret of the ultrarich and those with decades of experience. Author and investor David Greene holds nothing back, sharing the exact systems and processes he used to scale his business from buying two houses per year to buying two houses per month using BRRRR.

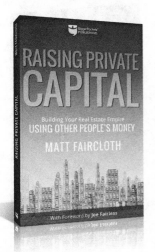

Raising Private Capital

Are you ready to help other investors build their wealth while you build your real estate empire? The road map outlined in *Raising Private Capital* helps investors looking to inject more private capital into their business—the most effective strategy for growth! Author and real estate investor Matt Faircloth shows you how to develop long-term wealth from his own valuable lessons and experiences in real estate. Get the truth behind the wins and losses from someone who has experienced it all.

More from
BiggerPockets Publishing

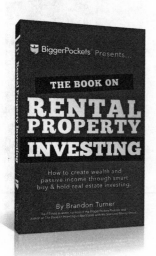

The Book on Rental Property Investing

The Book on Rental Property Investing by Brandon Turner, a real estate investor and cohost of the *BiggerPockets Podcast*, contains nearly 400 pages of in-depth advice and strategies for building wealth through rental properties. You will learn how to build an achievable plan, find incredible deals, pay for your rentals, and much more!

The Book on Flipping Houses, Revised Edition

Written by active real estate investor and fix-and-flipper J Scott, this book contains more than 300 pages of step-by-step training, perfect for both the complete newbie and the seasoned pro looking to build a house-flipping business. Whatever your skill level, this book will teach you everything you need to know to build a profitable business and start living the life of your dreams.

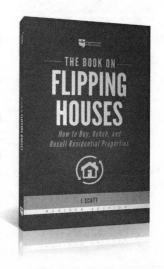

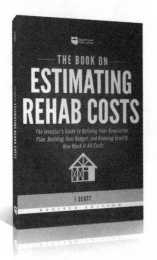

The Book on Estimating Rehab Costs, Revised Edition

Learn detailed tips, tricks, and tactics to accurately budget nearly any house-flipping project from expert fix-and-flipper J Scott. Whether you are preparing to walk through your very first rehab project or you're an experienced home flipper, this handbook will be your guide to identifying renovation projects, creating a scope of work, and staying on budget to ensure a timely profit!

The Book on Investing in Real Estate with No (and Low) Money Down

Lack of money holding you back from real estate success? It doesn't have to! In this groundbreaking book from Brandon Turner, author of *The Book on Rental Property Investing* and others, you'll discover numerous strategies investors can use to buy real estate using other people's money. You'll learn the top strategies that savvy investors are using to buy, rent, flip, or wholesale properties at scale!

CONNECT WITH BIGGERPOCKETS

and Become Successful in Your Real Estate Business Today!

Facebook
/BiggerPockets

Instagram
@BiggerPockets

Twitter
@BiggerPockets

LinkedIn
/company/Bigger
Pockets

Website
BiggerPockets.com